SONGS ON ENDLESS REPEAT

ALSO BY
ANTHONY VEASNA SO

Afterparties

SONGS ON ENDLESS REPEAT

Essays and Outtakes

ANTHONY VEASNA SO
FOREWORD BY JONATHAN DEE

ecco
An Imprint of HarperCollinsPublishers

Some of these pieces, as noted, are works of fiction. Names, characters, places, and incidents within these selections are products of the author's imagination or are used fictitiously, and are not to be construed as real. Any resemblance to actual events, locales, organizations, or persons, living or dead, is entirely coincidental.

SONGS ON ENDLESS REPEAT. Copyright © 2023 by Ravy So and Alexander Gilbert Torres. Foreword copyright © 2023 by Jonathan Dee. All rights reserved. Printed in the United States of America. No part of this book may be used or reproduced in any manner whatsoever without written permission except in the case of brief quotations embodied in critical articles and reviews. For information, address HarperCollins Publishers, 195 Broadway, New York, NY 10007.

HarperCollins books may be purchased for educational, business, or sales promotional use. For information, please email the Special Markets Department at SPsales@harpercollins.com.

Ecco® and HarperCollins® are trademarks of HarperCollins Publishers.

FIRST EDITION

Library of Congress Cataloging-in-Publication Data
Names: So, Anthony Veasna, 1992–2020, author.
Title: Songs on endless repeat : essays and outtakes / Anthony Veasna So.
Description: First edition. | New York, NY : Ecco, 2023.
Identifiers: LCCN 2023020569 (print) | LCCN 2023020570 (ebook) |
   ISBN 9780063049963 (hardcover) | ISBN 9780063049956 (ebook)
Subjects: LCGFT: Essays.
Classification: LCC PS3619.O33 S66 2023 (print) | LCC PS3619.O33 S66 2023
   (ebook) | DDC 814/.6—dc23/eng/20230608
LC record available at https://lccn.loc.gov/2023020569
LC ebook record available at https://lccn.loc.gov/2023020570

23 24 25 26 27 LBC 5 4 3 2 1

Several of these essays originally appeared, in slightly different form, in the following publications: *n+1* ("Journey to a Land Free of White People," "Baby Yeah"); *Ninth Letter* ("Manchester Street"); *The New Yorker* ("Duplex"); and *The Millions* ("A Year in Reading").

CONTENTS

FOREWORD BY JONATHAN DEE   IX

WE ARE ALL THE SAME HERE, US CAMBOS   1

MANCHESTER STREET   4

JOURNEY TO A LAND FREE OF WHITE PEOPLE   13

DEEP REALITY   25

PEOU AND HER KMOUYS   50

DARREN AND VINNY   58

A NOTE ON THE
HISTORY OF CAMBOTOWN FUNERALS   85

MOLLY (AND PEOU)   90

DUPLEX   118

A YEAR IN READING   138

THE ROSES   144

THE COUSINS AT THE FUNERAL   157

DINNER WITH THE CORE FAMILY   188

BABY YEAH   206

FOREWORD

"Also," Anthony emailed me in September of 2019, "I've figured out that I want my novel's style and prose and structure to be a cross between Helen Dewitt's *The Last Samurai*, Gabriel García Márquez's *One Hundred Years of Solitude*, and John Kennedy Toole's *A Confederacy of Dunces*. Of course there are other influences, but these three books are the ones that really jolt my creativity whenever I'm in a rut and need to read a passage to reignite me."

I'm not sure a word of *Straight Thru Cambotown* was written at that point. But the height of the bar he cheerfully set for himself, the ambition co-existing with the conscientiousness about acknowledging his debts, infuses not only my every memory of Anthony, but also every page he managed to write, in the brutally short time he had. The version of the novel you have before you is incomplete, of course, but that doesn't mean it's rough; reading it, I feel overwhelmed yet again by Anthony's deceptively casual, humor-cloaked command, the way in which writing itself was not simply a mode of expression for him, but his method of bringing into harness the sheer energy of his mind. He was one of the smartest people I've ever known. It was hard for him to stop thinking, to stop noticing. Every sentence seems at its observational bursting point.

But if intellect alone made great novelists, there would be a lot more of them. What stands out in *Straight Thru Cambotown*, just as in Anthony's brilliant debut story collection, *Afterparties*, is the particularity born of tenderness, the eye that misses nothing but forgives just about everything, the distinction between sentimentality and love. Anthony's fiction is a monument to the Cambodian American population in and around Stockton, California: its unique generational chasm, its sometimes overenthusiastic embrace of American excess, the struggle against forgetting versus the desire, sometimes the need, to forget. The genocide that produced this diasporic culture hovers over everything; Molly's unforgettable eulogy for her beloved Ming Peou reminds her audience, and us, that the ascendance of women like Peou in Cambo culture, however delightful or just in some aspects, will always rest upon the mass, generational murder of Cambodian men. Molly's cousin Darren—the character closest, in terms of surface detail, to Anthony himself—is home for the funeral from Stanford, where he's trying to write a graduate thesis that explains the relationship between "humor and trauma." *Straight Thru Cambotown* (originally Anthony's own graduate thesis at Syracuse University, where I was his teacher and adviser) is heartbreakingly smart on that score.

That's not to say he couldn't get righteously irritated, when the situation called for it. This volume also collects his published essays, some of them sweetly, almost protectively family-focused, and others, more critical in nature, on a range of mass-cultural topics, from *Queer Eye for the Straight Guy* as an avatar of what he calls "deep-reality TV" to the film *Crazy Rich Asians*, with which he felt himself in a kind of one-sided dialogue. (He frequently acted out this sort of friendly, wholly imaginary rivalry with other Asian and Asian American artists, always in a comic, self-needling way. He loved to refer to Viet Thanh Nguyen, for instance, as "my nemesis," followed immediately by a burst of laughter, the joke being that Viet Thanh Nguyen would of course not then have had the slightest hint of Anthony's existence.) The fact that these brilliantly funny, humbly astute works of criticism were, unlike the novel, finished products in Anthony's lifetime paradoxically makes them feel more truncated here—in the sense that, after reading them, you will, as does everyone who knew him, find yourself encountering some bizarre new cultural phenomenon and feeling first a curiosity, then a sort of enraged sadness, eager for the sense that Anthony would have made of it.

The alternating fiction and nonfiction sections of this book are in constant dialogue (in the meditations on queerness, on comedy, on music, on whiteness, etc.); the borderline fades, though, in the difficult final pages, when the subject on both planes turns to grief, and to the problem of how to mourn an untimely death. *Cambotown*, naturally, finds elements of humor in this process, however embedded in agony, as the extended family tries to figure out how to bear the loss of its eccentric matriarch. And in the essay that closes this volume, Anthony turns, as he always did, to the making of sentences as the only conceivable way of bringing under control the crippling pain he felt in the aftermath of the death of his friend, the poet Will Georges. "My friend and I," he remembers, "saw each other as hopeless writers, misunderstood prophets, critics of our cultural moment who rejected obvious and reductive politics. We never indulged the ordinary pursuits because we yearned to write masterpieces, timeless works infused with nihilistic joy and dissenting imaginations." His confused fury, in the wake of Will's death, spares no one, least of all himself.

It is hard to read, because of course it begins to converge with our own sense of grief and loss and anger as the pages of this book, Anthony's last, run out. Sometimes it just hits you, the way it hits Molly—knocks her to the ground, in fact—when a random association makes her realize all over again that her beloved Ming Peou is truly gone. But the day comes for all writers when the only aspect of us that retains the power of speech is our work; if that day came for Anthony much sooner than expected, it is still a mistake to dwell on what's not here, what he didn't do. As time passes, the fact that he left us with two completely unprecedented book-length works of genius, two books that plant Cambo culture forever on the literary map of America, will move closer to the fore of our thoughts about him. And we need every word of this book. He wasn't just another promising young writer; let's face it, promising young writers are never in short supply. Anthony was filling a hole. So let the focus rest on his work, where it now belongs. It's the only place left to put the love I have for him, and it more than returns that love.

—Jonathan Dee

SONGS ON ENDLESS REPEAT

WE ARE ALL THE SAME HERE, US CAMBOS

FICTION, FROM *STRAIGHT THRU CAMBOTOWN*

Just look around and listen to the talk. Him, her, them. Those fools over there blasting Tupac like they actually get it, because, in a way, beneath the yellow-brown-light-dark surface of their skin, they do. Then the Mings dishing out papaya salad with a portion of side-eye from their minivans in the park, which is both peaceful and sketchy, kid-friendly and stabby. Then the Bas chugging iced coffee with condensed milk before their second jobs as janitors or landscapers; the hopeful Mais trying, desperately, to teach their toddlers English without crashing too hard into the last syllable of each word; the Mas crowded in the one and only Cambo doctor's waiting room and complaining about the dumbass Khmer accents of their dumbass Americanized grandkids; the other Bas drinking and drinking with the Pous and Gongs to consume the years of their lives, Heineken for the humble, Hennessy for the ballers, both for those who give zero shits about good old-fashioned American opportunity;

and even the daughters and sons who are seriously over it, every goddamn thing, most of them trying to finish their degrees in accounting or physical therapy, or if they're smart enough, lucky enough, nursing. In Cambotown, we are all the same—same stories, same history. Or lack thereof.

Actually, to be more precise, it's easy to think we have the same story. We do, and we don't, but we mostly do. Though some people take our similarities too far, stretching them to include those we had never even encountered before coming to America. Look at a map and tell us why we get lumped together with the people of countries two thousand miles away from Cambodia. (We're all for more brothers and sisters, but what do we have in common with Koreans? Other than American, Soviet, and Chinese governments fighting their wars on our land, through our governments they helped corrupt, like we're sock puppets used to act out marital problems in couples therapy? Seriously, we don't even eat the same grain of rice!)

Ask anyone here, and they'll give you the same taglines: Early '70s is civil war and coups d'état. Late '70s is Communist-style book burning, entire libraries up in flames, and killing fields ornamented with piles of skulls everywhere. Early '80s is refugee camps and immigration and adopting new names such as Steve, Bill, and Kathy, names we always forget to use, names we didn't realize were nicknames for longer names such as Steven, William, and Catherine. Late '80s is overdosing on fresh-off-the-skillet perms and Tom Cruise aviator sunglasses and gangs, gang violence, and gang wars with other gangs, mostly Hispanic. Early '90s is, okay, still gangs, but also small business owners and the American

Dream of grocery stores that stock and restock fish sauce, while late '90s onward is PTSD symptoms passed down to kids like your mom's eyes and your dad's bad karma and your dead Gong's fat head, or what sure looks like a fat head from the single surviving photo of him pre-genocide.

And so on, you get the point. We're all the same. A lot of us even have the same birthdate, if you look at history a certain way. Remember when Pol Pot declared 1975 to be Year Zero? Sometimes our minds are too rattled to conceive of anything else.

That's why we'll never leave this place, not truly. We surrendered to the taglines, the shared sense of thinking—did that mind-boggling shit really happen? Oh, it did, it really did. Here's some coconut rice and a welfare check to make you feel better. Still, we're here, been here for years, and now we're sober of all that individualism bullshit. We're with you, have always been so. Let's be messed-up Cambos together.

MANCHESTER STREET

```
            NONFICTION,
 ORIGINALLY PUBLISHED IN NINTH LETTER
```

I want to give you, everyone in my audience, some words of advice. Never eat twenty dollars' worth of fast food at 4 p.m. and then immediately take a nap when it is 104 degrees outside, because when I did that, I had an absolutely fucked-up dream. I woke up in a panic and sweaty all over, even in the most obscure places of my body, from a dream where my dead grandparents came to me and screamed, "We did not die in a genocide so that you could pass out in the middle of the day after eating twenty tacos from Jack in the Box!"

Manchester was a neighborhood that consisted of one apartment complex residing three blocks south of two shopping malls. In the 1980s, the American government granted citizenship to Cambodian refugees, opening the Central Valley's floodgates for families to pour into the California Delta land and be corralled into cockroach-infested apartments in Manchester. Back then, the street resembled a primordial province of Cambodia more than an apartment complex in America. Its decaying concrete infrastructure seemed mere minutes away from collapsing, tired mothers stood outside washing heaps of laundry by hand, and every window was connected to the next by a bundle of wires that split one cable subscription twenty separate ways. Even Manchester's surrounding streets retained a look of another, more primitive world, encircling the neighborhood with fields of dead yellow grass growing wildly on plots of land that were, for some reason, cursed barren. But cockroaches be damned, this was the American Dream, and Manchester was still only three blocks away from two shopping malls.

My family, by which I mean my father's mother, his siblings, and all subsequent spouses tethered down to my patriarchal bloodline, lived in Manchester before my birth. By the time I was born in 1992, they had clawed their way out of poverty, and for the first decade of my life, we lived in humble middle-class homes, away from Manchester. Here, my parents, aunts, and uncles all prioritized English over Khmer, their native language, in an effort to ensure the academic futures of my cousins and me, buying us hoards of books, including already outdated paper encyclopedias, and putting on sophisticated television shows like *Frasier*.

We were also enrolled in a magnet school, the best our city had to offer. The daily routine of six kids of three different families all using the same fake address to qualify as in-district became a thirty-minute drive to a bus stop, a sixty-minute bus ride to school, five hours of instruction, a sixty-minute bus ride back to the same bus stop, a forty-five-minute walk to the public library, and a three-hour wait for someone to finally pick us up. At home, our parents stressed over their finances, figuring out more ways to shatter ceilings and prevent plateaus, accumulating more equity and more property to support their children, who stressed over performance in classwork, instructions for homework, avoidance of late work, complete reading comprehension, standardized testing deviation, long division of multiplication, pristine penmanship when writing calligraphic cursive, color-coated project boards for oral presentations, perfect utilization of the creative right-sided brain, brilliant maximization of precocious logical inducements, hypochondriac tendencies from attendance paranoia, and anything else that proved everything was fucking worth it. All to cultivate our potential genius, our potential success, our future life of ease.

All our parents could do was push us. Their never-ending states of anxiety and associate's degrees ill-equipped them to help us with things such as geometry or five-paragraph essays, leaving us alone to blindly navigate the American school system. We were left with lights that only lit up to the grade level of our oldest cousin. Luckily, we found refuge at the public library, a cheap daycare stocked with books to pave the way to an education higher than our parents' alma mater, Delta Community College, which so many other Manchester Cambodians started and never finished, even if it was their only option. The library let us lose ourselves in the fantasy of Narnia, Uriel, and Hogwarts, reach for hope hidden in giant peaches and glass elevators by Roald Dahl, and then spout along to the witticisms of Holden Caulfield. We spent afternoons flipping pages until one of our parents reached the maximum amount of paid hours their jobs allowed.

By my prepubescence, it was clear that we had great academic futures, so our parents didn't need to worry. Nevertheless, satisfaction is foreign to their nature, and our parents soon recalibrated their concern to scrutinize our ignorance of the Khmer words and Cambodian customs we were forced to turn our backs on while studying at the school desk of American education. Instead of analyzing children's literature, we listened to tales of the olden days in Cambodia. Instead of memorizing mathematical algorithms, we counted spoonfuls of whatever Cambodian dish flavored with fermented fish paste our parents tried acclimating us to that day.

For all our academic promise, we still fell short, berated for what couldn't have been our fault. It was impossible to satisfy our parents, and this sentiment recycled itself over and over again into the present, where our parents criticize us for being nowhere close to marriage after forbidding relationships all throughout our education. They condemn dating while condoning marriage, setting us up for failure, again. All our parents do is push us. Pushing toward America, pushing for advancement. Pushing against America, pushing for preservation. Going this way and that way, finding faults with everything, because nothing's right and nothing fits. We need to constantly push to find some satisfaction in this society. But survival is all we can do, perpetually pushing on, afraid to stop, because what the hell would we do, then?

I'm going to teach you some of the only Khmer words I know. It is "amuy nou." It literally means "that guy." It is the only thing I've ever heard my parents use to refer to my sister's white boyfriend. They've been dating for five years.

What haunted our parents the most was the premonition that our native language would cease to exist in future generations. Thence, they enrolled us in the Khmer school held at Manchester. Every Saturday morning, six kids were dropped off at the gates of the ghetto for school that wasn't really school. Classes were held inside an abandoned daycare stuck in a barely used courtyard. Our Khmer teachers weren't really teachers but, rather, translators hired by the school districts and promoted to teachers by prideful relatives. Here in Manchester, translators were teachers, Hondas were Mustangs, Olive Gardens were fine dining, all colleges outside the Central Valley were UC Berkeley, and being babysat by bilingual Cambodian Americans in their thirties was Khmer School.

We began classes and immediately realized that the other students were already fluent, a skill that couldn't be attributed to our teachers, whose philosophies of education consisted mostly of worksheets that tested how well we used the process of elimination. No, our classmates had learned Khmer simply by growing up in Manchester, a place filled with parents who didn't bother climbing the socioeconomic pyramid that requires proficient English, grandmothers whose jobs consisted of convincing social workers of their ongoing disabilities, men that only made enough money to book flights to Cambodia and impress their poorer relatives while wooing their pregnant mistresses, girls that never took advantage of the free pills from Planned Parenthood, boys that flowed into gangs like rain down a sewer drain, and kids that gave up their dreams before they learned about student loans—all with their own culture inside those iron bar gates.

My cousins and I had never felt less Cambodian in our lives, and learning Khmer wouldn't have changed the fact that we had almost nothing in common with the inhabitants of Manchester. Even our blood was less Cambodian, the one Chinese ancestor we had lightening our complexions to mark us as different at first glance. Our classmates called us "Chinese" instead of "Cambodian." To them, our "Chinese" blood was the reason for our difference in intelligence and socioeconomic class. And we made no effort to step past these differences. We rushed through our handouts and never talked, letting our teachers think we were painfully shy rather than unable to answer back in Khmer. We sat among ourselves, whispering about the lack of basic necessities like air-conditioning and scented hand soaps. We stole glances at the clock, waiting for the inevitable return to our comfortable middle-class existence. We stayed on our side of the room, and our classmates stayed on theirs.

After a couple of months, my cousins and I were re-enrolled for the more intensive summer program. By now, our parents didn't expect us to become fluent in Khmer, as our excellent grades at regular school, combined with our inability to understand the language, proved that Khmer school wasn't the most legitimate institution, but at ten dollars a month, it had replaced the library as the cheapest babysitter around. Saturdays thus turned into all week; mornings, into eight hours a day, which is a fucking long time for kids to sit in near silence. There was literally nothing to do but let the seemingly endless amount of time together corrode the cultural barrier between our classmates and us. So, we all fell into friendship, like kids so easily do in the summer.

It was hard growing up Cambodian American. With no one to look up to except our parents. If you look at the media now, other races have great role models. Look at Barack Obama: he's fun, he's cool. Cambodian people, we only have Angelina Jolie's Cambodian adopted son, Maddox. Maddox Jolie Pitt. And sometimes he really is my role model, because I'm still waiting for a rich white person to adopt me.

Mondays were the only days our teachers tried teaching, renewed with false hope they somehow cultivated over the weekend. By Tuesday, they'd given up on any delusions of academic grandeur. We were given the rest of the week to explore, allowed to ramble around Manchester with no one to supervise where we went and whom we met.

Every apartment contained a pop-up business managed by entrepreneurial parents, making Manchester not unlike a Sunday flea market or canopied bazaar. Some apartments sold Doritos, Snickers, and Marlboros bought wholesale at Costco. Others offered cosmetic services without the proper credentials and competence. Entire bedrooms were dedicated to assembly lines of older matrons that manufactured commissioned Cambodian novelties, like Buddhist prayer mats and wooden dancing Apsaras. Living rooms were antique stores. Closets were pawn shops. Anything was on sale for the right price. We blew cash on knockoff Pokémon cards and other collectibles, rummaging through the belongings of children with unsympathetic parents, choosing between handmade action figures symbolizing Cambodian iconography to show our Caucasian friends and further confuse them about our heritage. We dined at the makeshift noodle shop in Apartment 23C because it had the fewest number of kitchen cockroaches. My cousins and I relished the freedom to satisfy any junk food cravings or buy any useless toys, while our classmates kept their hands in their empty pockets. They only introduced us to each vendor, unknowingly playing their part in that marketplace instilled by their parents. But for all the illegitimate practices and unnoteworthy profits, these enterprises still maintained an infinite longevity, a foolproof business plan: no amount of auditing would ever uncover any untaxed profits, as the paper trail left by any questionable merchandising consisted of nothing more than the welfare checks stuffed into the mailbox each month. Government money flew into Manchester and never came out, like half of the Cambodians living there.

Every week was the same—the same junk foods, the same lesson plans, the same people. We played with the same great-grandchildren crawling around, unable to distinguish between baby noises and actual Khmer words. The teenage boys always leaned on the northward wall while smoking their fathers' Marlboros, spending all day cultivating lung cancer and planning various crimes to commit after the sun set. The same cranky dads tried to sleep before their graveyard shifts. The same irritable moms with too many generations to feed snapped at their rigid mothers-in-law, grandmothers who made the smell of incense a permanent fixture throughout Manchester. They spent all day chanting along to chain-smoking monks that visited from the Buddhist temple. If you weren't careful, you could be locked in a room of elderly Cambodian women who banned any movement except to participate in a synchronized bow. The mats they sat on for hours at a time imprinted your bare legs with throbbing lashes. The pain of diligent praying and the loss of hope for the present was the price for a better, reincarnated life.

At the end of every week, our cravings waned. The junk food we had relished earlier in the week became unappetizing. The sugar rush faded. We dropped down to our reality, where we felt the burden of claustrophobic apartments without air-conditioning. We started to look forward to the weekend, planning out what video games we would play and what cartoons we would watch, while our classmates discussed their own weekend plans doing who knows what. On Fridays, we compulsively checked the time until our parents came driving down the street. We would never leave right away, though. Our parents always started their weekends by walking deep into the apartment complex to chat with their old friends, reminiscing about exotic fruits found only in Cambodian memory. These conversations always felt like an eternity. And we were always impatient, even if we knew our visit to Manchester would end soon enough.

JOURNEY TO A LAND FREE OF WHITE PEOPLE

NONFICTION, ORIGINALLY PUBLISHED IN n+1

The day the *Crazy Rich Asians* trailer premiered online, I watched it on repeat for an hour. Then I watched it a dozen more times, texting a series of half-formed thoughts to a group chat with my three Asian American writer friends. I'd spent the previous year joking that the four of us needed to have our novels ready to sell the day *Crazy Rich Asians* was released, right at the stroke of midnight. I'd even urged them to join CrossFit, so that we could all confront our breakout literary stardom and our author photos with hard bodies. If *Crazy Rich Asians* proved to be a hit, studio heads and publishing hotshots would buy up Asian American stories the way my aunt buys dollar flip-flops during Old Navy's annual flip-flop sale—in a delirious, short-lived mania. If it failed, we'd have to start studying for the LSATs.

This was and wasn't hyperbole. Ever since the film's announcement, and especially [since] the news about its all-Asian cast—in addition to the controversy over Henry

Golding's biracial background, one producer originally wanted Constance Wu's protagonist, Rachel Chu, to be rewritten into a white role for a white female—I've found it close to impossible to avoid what the internet calls "the discourse." A quick Google search months before the movie even premiered would have inundated you with think pieces and Twitter reaction roundups ranging from "'Crazy Rich Asians' Isn't Just a Movie—It's a Sign That I Matter, Too" to "An All-Asian Cast and No Martial Arts: Why the 'Crazy Rich Asians' Movie Matters" to "The Trailer for 'Crazy Rich Asians' Has Some Asking: Where Are the Brown Faces?" to "Ben Baller Thinks 'Crazy Rich Asians' Is Going to Set Asians Back 40 Years, Sparks Debate" to "No, 'Crazy Rich Asians' Isn't the Asian 'Black Panther.'" (I might get my woke card revoked for saying this, but I think the *Crazy Rich Asians–Black Panther* comparison is useful, insofar as both films attempt to reimagine societies from the perspective of a race marginalized in the United States, where white people *appear* to have almost zero relevance, in ways that are culturally specific to their respective races.) Over the past year, the ever-churning hype machine transformed *Crazy Rich Asians* into a make-or-break moment for Asian American media representation, and many people of different backgrounds bought into the hype—at least according to their Twitter feeds. Paradoxically, the appeal of the novel from which *Crazy Rich Asians* was adapted was its promise of reprieve from the never-ending battle of racism, yet the discourse surrounding the film has sought to place it somewhere—anywhere—on a barometer of political progress.

As much as I might have wanted to situate myself outside this conversation, it was impossible. I don't live in a cave. It would have been foolish not to be excited about the biggest Asian American movie produced by a major studio since *The Joy Luck Club*, which was released in 1993, a year after I was born. So, by the time the trailer was uploaded to YouTube, my expectations for it—much less the movie—were high. It would either blow my mind and inspire me with its exuberant diversity or enrage and offend me due to its total political failure. Supporting or rejecting this movie as an Asian American would be a complicated and tumultuous affair, like loving your tone-deaf grandparents while hating the idea of going out with them in public.

The most surprising thing about the trailer was that I turned out not to have any strong feelings about it at all. I spent over an hour failing to be provoked in any particular direction. In my group chat, my three friends questioned my fixation on what they deemed to be not much more than advertising, but I didn't understand how we could avoid reading too much into the trailer. The film's production details, cast interviews, and promotional materials have spurred as much debate as the film itself. Trailers may not be filmic truth, but it's impossible to pretend they don't exist. And, in my case, impossible not to watch them over and over again.

What the trailer suggested, above all, was a movie dead set on coasting. It looked funny enough, but never more than that, and many of its punch lines fell flat. (What was hilarious about the moment when Henry Golding smirks and declares that he's more of a Prince Harry rather than a Prince William? It was a line begging for a laugh track.)

The set design and the costumes were brash and opulent, yet somehow everything looked plainer than it should have. It just wasn't dynamic enough to live up to the hype, and the conventional framing and editing seemed to undermine what should've been "crazy." While the cast in the trailer was, as promised, the most Asian I'd seen in an American movie—and all this without samurais or martial arts moves or corny accents—the omnipresence of fair-skinned model types rendered the diversity more lukewarm than bracing. (Also, the Singaporean characters' posh English pronunciation was almost as grating as Hollywood's grotesque array of bad "Asian" speech patterns.) Every text I sent to my chat was muddled. I wavered constantly between admiration and criticism, support and rejection. Several times, I texted a punch line from the trailer verbatim, along with "Is this funny? I think so but I can't tell." I felt preemptively let down and a little sheepish about the intensity of my fervor.

I'd also had mixed feelings about the source material when I read it a couple of years ago, before the movie was announced. The *Crazy Rich Asians* novel is an entertaining yet shallow read, refreshing to the extent that it has no patience for the melancholic Asian American literary tradition. But I couldn't get down with the way Kevin Kwan went about undermining the model minority myth. (Clearly, I wasn't one of the Asians discussed in an *Atlantic* article titled "Why Asians Love 'Crazy Rich Asians.'") Kwan delights in dismantling stereotypes, but he doesn't have much aim or consistency, and his approach is zero-sum: anytime one character does something dynamic and unexpected, other characters get flattened into reductive caricatures. The male lead character Nick Young's sexy Prince Charming persona successfully subverts the stereotype of Asian men as effeminate and passive, but in order to emphasize Nick's appeal, Kwan forces the female protagonist, Rachel Chu, to perform the function of the pitiful Asian American woman who has never once dated an Asian American man—who has spurned them throughout her life, only to be converted by Nick's suaveness. (This aspect of the novel's characterization of Rachel feels like wish fulfillment for someone who read the introduction to Frank Chin, Jeffery Paul Chan, Lawson Fusao Inada, and Shawn Wong's *Aiiieeeee! An Anthology of Asian American Writers* and cheered when the editors throw Asian women who marry white men under the bus).

But, finally, months after I started torturing myself via sustained exposure to the trailer on YouTube, I saw *Crazy Rich Asians*. Sitting in a half-empty theater in the second-biggest mall in America—aptly named Destiny USA—I was surprised by how emotional I felt. The experience of the trailer dissipated. I thought of my friends and family and wished we were all watching this movie together. Nothing could match the tenderness I felt watching a party scene with a large group of Asian American characters that evoked many of—though, to be fair, nowhere near all—the wildly different aunts, uncles, cousins and second cousins I grew up around. The challenge was to revel in all this deep feeling while taking seriously the film's faults and ill-conceived symbolism—and, perhaps, its political utility for the Asian American diaspora.

—

CRAZY RICH ASIANS MIGHT BEST be described as a big-tent romantic comedy. It makes plenty of room for a multigenerational family saga, a modern-day fairy tale, a domestic marital drama, a satirical comedy of manners, a slapstick farce, and an epic heroic journey. There are catty asides and subtle and not-so-subtle power plays, farcical set pieces and relationship turmoil. The director, Jon M. Chu; the writers, Peter Chiarelli and Adele Lim; and the entire cast turned *Crazy Rich Asians* into a Trojan horse for all the unmade Asian American movies audiences have missed out on their entire lives.

Which is not to say that the film successfully delivers on the potential of all these genres. But the disparate narrative threads, in all their fumbling glory, parallel the heterogenous nature of the Asian and Asian American world. What better way to represent Asian diversity—if, that is, you aren't actually representing or telling the stories of a diverse array of Asian ethnicities—than to make an Asian American movie filled with clashing tones and genres?

The film's genres map onto its four central female characters. (Most of the male characters, particularly Henry Golding as the leading man, remain boring and one-dimensional—the creators managed to depict Asian men as attractive, sexual beings rather than effeminate nerds, it's true, but they forgot to give them personalities, reducing them to little more than beautiful shells.) Constance Wu's Rachel Chu, an American-born Chinese game theory professor at New York University, travels to Singapore for the first time to meet her rich boyfriend Nick Young's entire family and to attend the Singaporean wedding of the year. Rachel's Singaporean best friend from college, Peik Lin—played with hilarious abandon by Awkwafina—lives a new-money life in Singapore that barely overlaps with Nick's élite old-money world. Gemma Chan's Astrid Leong-Teo, Nick's favorite cousin, spends most of the movie conflicted about her husband's adultery. And, finally, there's Eleanor Sung-Young, Nick's formidable, traditional, and endlessly classy mother, who views Rachel as "not being from the right type of people" and, thus, wrong for her son. Michelle Yeoh's performance as Eleanor is tight-lipped intensity incarnate.

At times, Peik Lin, Astrid, and Eleanor embody so many different, non-overlapping affects and tones [that] they appear to operate in completely separate movies. Peik Lin steamrolls through her scenes as the film's one genuinely funny character, as resplendent as her bright-pink Audi, which zigzags through Singapore's freeways at an ungodly speed. Watching her transform every slight movement into an opportunity for physical comedy, you almost forget that *Crazy Rich Asians* isn't a funnier and sharper version of itself—a satire of élite Singaporean society. Astrid, her husband, and their marital issues, meanwhile, are the killjoy melodramatic foil to the movie's other storylines—a humorless domestic drama trapped inside a comedy. Astrid's scenes unfold in hushed tones; dark, melancholic blues; and shadowy cinematography—a stark contrast to the rest of the movie's eye-popping brightness. Eleanor remains intensely focused on derailing her son's relationship with Rachel, who is deemed too American and low-class to marry into the Young family. Yeoh is so good that Eleanor's grandiose drama of family legacy verges on the persuasive, despite the lack of context for why it's so important for this family to retain its traditions in the first place, other than they've been rich since the 1800s. (The family's main traditions: be rich, make dumplings, marry rich, have parties, look fabulous.) From the boisterous mess of these characters and their clashing genres emerges Rachel Chu, the film's one truly Asian American character, the hero of this journey to a foreign land free of white people.

Crazy Rich Asians marks Rachel as different, a true individual who indulges in good food and plays a mean game of poker and possesses a heroic origin story: she grew up with a poor single mom, worked her way up to becoming the youngest faculty member at NYU, and has a secret broken past waiting to be revealed. We watch as Rachel's mother, after giving advice on dealing with traditional Chinese families, tells Rachel, "Your face is Chinese, you speak Chinese," and then, pointing at Rachel's head and heart, warns her, "but here and here, you're different." We watch as Rachel tries to prove herself to Nick's family as something more than a "banana [that's] yellow on the outside and white on the inside," while Eleanor and everyone else in Nick's orbit subjects her to various enhanced interrogation techniques: eye rolls, a mutilated squid, a private investigator. Then, as the movie progresses, we come to realize how this "difference" Rachel possesses—this cultural hybridity—actually affirms her integrity. In this way, we are made to understand that Rachel is our Asian American hero, someone who can merge the movie's disparate narrative threads—and all the fragments of the Asian and Asian American world—into a cohesive whole. Dressed in floral print after floral print (plus a baby-blue Cinderella gown adorned with fabric flowers), in contrast to Astrid's and Eleanor's muted colors and sleek silhouettes, Rachel symbolizes the spring awakening for a unified Asian identity.

There was something exhilarating about watching Rachel, a dynamic Asian American female character, go up against the antagonistic but complicated Eleanor, while the men of the movie spent their time enmeshed in cringe-worthy conversations and easy punch lines. (I'm still trying to forget that bachelor party yacht scene and Nick's cousin Alistair yelling that Rachel has small breasts.) But the way Rachel goes about ushering in a new era of unified Asian-hood left me uneasy.

In three pivotal monologues throughout the movie, Rachel announces her cultural and socioeconomic upbringing to Eleanor and other characters, a reminder to the audience of the way she's been coded as different, of her status as an underdog hero to root for. The first time Rachel and Eleanor meet, in one of the film's clunkier moments of dialogue, Rachel jumps into a monologue about her background after forcing Eleanor into a hug. She tells her that her mom emigrated from China when Rachel was still a baby, how she didn't finish school but fought her way up from poverty to become one of the top real estate agents in Flushing, Queens. The chaos of the kitchen obstructs Rachel's attempts to be heard, and Eleanor ignores Rachel's oversharing. Once the monologue is over, Eleanor dismisses Rachel's decision to pursue her passion and career, something Eleanor considers a vulgar American antithesis to the Singaporean "tradition" of building family. Later, while making traditional dumplings with Nick's immediate family, Rachel reiterates that she and her mom had no family support during her childhood. Here again, Eleanor interprets the monologue as evidence that Rachel's upbringing has not taught her to prioritize family above her own passions. Eleanor proceeds to tell Rachel that "she will never be enough" for Nick.

After these failed attempts to be *recognized*, Rachel pierces through Eleanor's classist condemnation in a showdown that literally happens over a game of mahjong. Eleanor and the audience listen as Rachel, determined to say her last piece, her expression full of grit, acceptance, and heartbreak, explains her reasons for rejecting Nick's marriage proposal. As the women play mahjong in seamless, calculated moves, Rachel says that she doesn't want to marry Nick if it means taking him away from his mother, again communicating to Eleanor that she knows that Nick lived with his Ah-Ma as a child, a sacrifice Eleanor made to ensure Nick's status in the family. But then, as she knowingly forfeits a mahjong tile that allows Eleanor to play a winning hand, Rachel asserts that in the future, when Nick has grandchildren, Eleanor will have to grapple with the fact that her whole "traditional" world only exists because of the actions of a "poor, raised-by-a-single-mother, low-class immigrant nobody." Donned, yet again, in a floral print dress, one decorated in tree branches blooming red, pink, and yellow flowers, Rachel demonstrates to Eleanor that she has *allowed* her to win, both in the mahjong game and in their conflict over the handsome and unremarkable Nick.

Here, Rachel's declaration of identity is at last *heard* by Eleanor. This last monologue prompts Eleanor to give Nick her own wedding ring, a symbol of her acceptance, so that he can, in full rom-com trope mode, propose to Rachel on an airplane. Which leads directly to the final scene of the movie, an engagement party for Rachel and Nick where every Asian character gathers to celebrate this union of East and West, tradition and modernity, every genre, tone, and storyline the movie checks off. Floating above Singapore on a rooftop garden bridging three skyscrapers, this party scene represents the new Asian world Rachel has brought forth, one so coherent, resolute, and unified that the synchronized swimmers who perform routines in the background can't help but feel symbolic.

But what are we supposed to do with all this? Are we, as actual participators in the political landscape, supposed to buy into the idea that the mere announcement and subsequent acknowledgment of Rachel's identity has the symbolic power to unify the heterogenous characters of this Asian and Asian American society? Are vocalization and acceptance strong enough to resolve political tensions and reconcile cultural contradictions, such as Eleanor's adherence to a Singaporean "tradition" that is—somehow—at once diametrically opposed to Rachel's Western upbringing and structured by Western capitalist and colonialist influence? (The first time we see Eleanor, she is conducting a Bible study group, and every character and their mom went to Oxford or Cambridge.) The answer is obviously no. The recognition of difference isn't potent enough to dismantle harmful cultural institutions. And a very American form of individualism—embodied by our hero—is unlikely to bring about a progressive future.

By funneling its chaotic jumble of characters and genres into tenuous coherence, *Crazy Rich Asians* ends up as a lukewarm reminder that we should embrace those different from us rather than [as] a gloriously messy celebration of a huge population's heterogenous population. Still, watching *Crazy Rich Asians* upend its promise of diverse representation is politically useful. The film's misguided ending mirrors the grandiose claims of praise and rejection commentators have made on its behalf. On one hand, Rachel's triumphant assertion of her identity parallels the inflated idea that *Crazy Rich Asians* can dismantle barriers just because it features an all-Asian cast and people will watch it—that representation in and of itself is always powerful. On the other, to be too strident in one's criticism of the film's politics is to buy into the idea that there could be some great work of art, some truly "authentic" representation, some hero like Rachel, who might bring us the enlightened future we deserve. To accept or reject a story implies a standard that needs to be met, but how else can we continually revise our standards without accepting stories like *Crazy Rich Asians* as they are? *Crazy Rich Asians* might not be an authentic portrayal of our world, but it conveys enough truth to show us our own biases. In the end, that's more than enough.

DEEP REALITY

NONFICTION

The youngest of our adults have never known a cultural landscape not saturated and informed by reality television. Just as most college freshmen and sophomores were born after September 11, anyone who cannot legally drink in the United States is predated by *Survivor* and *Big Brother*.

There are a number of ways I could have arrived at this obvious-in-retrospect conclusion. I could have dwelled on the fact that as a queer man of color, I sometimes feel irresponsible and ashamed whenever I don't attend a *RuPaul's Drag Race* viewing party at one of the dozen gay bars within walking distance of my San Francisco apartment (even though I barely watch the show). I could have spent a few seconds thinking about how, when I was teaching high school English a few years ago, several of my students performed an original one-act play about *Survivor*, in which three cast members get stranded in the ocean, forgotten by their CBS production crew. The play's transcendentalist theme of social isolation alone made it clear that *Survivor* has become the subject of teenage nostalgic projection. Or, of course, I could have simply noticed the countless reality TV shows currently on the air, each new hit spawning spin-offs and variations and rip-off versions like patient zero before the apocalypse.

But it was at Destiny USA—the giant mall-city crossbreed in Syracuse, New York—that I truly came to my senses. A friend and I were walking around Macy's when we encountered a life-sized, Lauren Conrad–shaped advertisement for Lauren Conrad's makeup line. I'm a longtime fan of *Laguna Beach* and *The Hills*, but even I was surprised that Lauren was still relevant enough to sell products at such a literal large scale. My friend, only three years younger than me, said that he had no idea who Lauren Conrad was, though he knew he recognized her from somewhere. All this after *Family Guy* dedicated an entire episode to her called "We Love You, Conrad"!

I found it unsettling that this super-famous person—or, at least, super-famous to me—could be familiar to my friend the way Hollywood celebrities of a certain age attain a degree of universal, nonspecific familiarity. He didn't know Lauren's backstory, had no clue how she'd become a fashion mogul, but he didn't have to. It was strange to think that a former reality TV star no longer needed to be fully known to have relevance, that she could be the face, and not just owner, of a bestselling department store brand, alongside Keira Knightley for Chanel and Eva Longoria for L'Oréal.

It became clear to me at that moment that reality television had outgrown its ostentatious phase, that it had transcended its status as a blip in pop-cultural history and settled into its current status as a natural element of our mundane existence. The genre has entrenched itself into our lives. We no longer question, or even notice, its presence. We have mindlessly accepted its influence.

—

MY ENCOUNTER WITH LAUREN CONRAD'S giant face in Destiny USA occurred in August 2018. Two months later, I found myself at an event sponsored by Syracuse University featuring Antoni Porowski, one of *Queer Eye*'s Fab Five— along with Tan, Karamo, Bobby, and Jonathan. The event had no real exigency. No cultural holiday was attached to Antoni's visit—not National Coming Out Day or Pride or even Canada Day. No theme of marginalization, belonging, or queer representation was underscored, and anyway, it's well known that the university's central obligation is to avoid being exclusionary to the straights. It was Homecoming Weekend, so I guess that was why he was there, though I couldn't detect an obvious connection between Antoni and college football.

The event was packed. My one gay friend in Syracuse had reserved me a ticket. We sat in the upstairs balcony, where we encountered several other gay male adults, while the downstairs mezzanine was packed with undergraduates, mostly hordes of sorority-type women and their token gay best friends, all of whom were yelling at the top of their lungs because *the* Antoni—food and wine expert, walking thirst trap—was gracing them with his presence. There was a mutual understanding among the gay adults on the balcony. We couldn't deny that Antoni *was* attractive as a man and a social form, but we wanted to keep our distance. Despite the "queer" in *Queer Eye*, we were not Antoni's audience. I had decided to bring poppers to sniff because—and here I'm quoting myself—"Someone needs to actually *be* queer in this auditorium."

His hair gelled into a severe side part, Antoni was wearing ripped black skinny jeans, a punk graphic T-shirt, and a leather jacket at once oversized and tightly fitted, so stiff it looked like it should have never left a fashion shoot. Antoni's enthusiasm was bubbly, if robotic, his opening "Yaaassssssssss!" like something he was reading off cue cards. He then launched into a set of snappy one-liners about the audience, the city, and the resemblance of the local vegan restaurant's sesame noodles to those found at Trader Joe's, which particularly irked me, as the son of a car repair mechanic and shop owner—why throw a small business under the bus of a corporate grocery chain? Antoni seemed like he was trying on different celebrity personas. He was the edgy queer, the feisty queer, the effervescent queer. The result was uncanny, a disaster of conflicting personalities, a human android malfunctioning because he was being ordered to do and be too many things at once.

High off poppers, I watched the student moderator call ten students to the stage, all of whom lined up by gender—five men to Antoni's right, five women to his left. The guest of honor would announce the university's homecoming king and queen. The winners were a fraternity boy and sorority girl who used to date and were now being crowned, awkwardly, by a TV star. Both winners were so conventional-looking that their total sum of remarkable features was net negative;

the only noteworthy thing was the way the boy's lanky height made it apparent that Antoni was much shorter than advertised—but then, that was obvious from watching any of the episodes. One of the finalists for homecoming king was a gender-bending, male-presenting student in ten-inch stilettos and sheer black stockings that ran all the way up to their black corset top. Antoni completely ignored them.

The rest of the event consisted of Antoni teaching the newly appointed homecoming king and queen how to make a carrot salad. This involved peeling and cutting several carrots, throwing in a large handful of raisins and nuts, and mixing a dressing out of olive oil, orange zest, and salt and pepper. During the Q&A that followed, several students in the audience lined up to ask questions that had been screened by Antoni's manager. *How do you remain so positive? What was your big break? How did you find your passion?* None of Antoni's answers are worth mentioning here. The whole event struck me as blatant, distilled, unashamed homonormativity. I felt embarrassed to be there, and by our similar names, and by the fact that when I took a "Which 'Queer Eye' Guy Are You?" quiz online one time, I got Antoni.

I didn't think much of any of this until the following spring, when a student in the undergraduate composition class I was teaching mentioned her love for *Queer Eye*. I asked her what she thought of the Antoni Porowski event. "I loved it," she said. "He's just such a *nice* person."

"Well, isn't that the bare minimum of what people should be?" I responded. "*Nice*. It doesn't seem like that should be applauded, and it definitely isn't something that makes anyone interesting."

The conversation escalated. The Antoni student argued that Antoni was indeed interesting, and her classmates began to chime in to second her opinions. This went on for a while—obviously, many of my students wanted to kill class time—until I declared, sternly, that Antoni has zero real personality. Of course, this implied—unintentionally!—that I thought the Antoni student also had zero personality. The Antoni student was offended. Still, it was clear that instead of engaging with challenging ideas, or ideas that had the remote possibility of being challenging, these students had cast their lot with niceness.

At the end of the semester, one of my anonymous class surveys ended with "Anthony wasn't open to our ideas." Based on the handwriting, I am certain this was the Antoni student. She was probably right, but not about *Queer Eye*.

—

PERHAPS BECAUSE I RECENTLY FINISHED a year of teaching undergraduates at Syracuse University, my salary the kind of abysmal to force existential thoughts, I've been thinking about the emergence of a new subset of educational entertainment, its existence made possible by the ever-expanding, and now inconspicuous, omnipresence of reality TV, as well as by the rise of streaming platforms run by tech sociopaths and the collective decisions of fellow sociopaths at media organizations and entertainment conglomerates, all of whom have determined that, yes, what audiences want is to be inundated by as many viewing options as possible that blur together into one infinite scroll. Netflix is the epicenter of what one might call—and what I in fact will call—deep reality TV.

Cooking documentaries that supposedly examine different cultures in sensitive and illuminating ways—shows like *Ugly Delicious* and *Chef's Table*—are deep reality TV. So is *Dating Around*, along with the classy, noncompetitive yet still competitive etiquette of *The Final Table* and *The Great British Baking Show*.* I still remember watching *The Great British Baking Show*, for the first time, while tripping on acid. (It occurs to me that it may be this, and not teaching, that is the actual reason I have been fixating so much on reality TV.) My friend had described the show as "calming," and I just couldn't understand what that meant. The show's affectless narrative momentum repressed any normal sense of competition—how was that calming? I found it claustrophobic, almost passive-aggressive, and I also couldn't stand that no one in the show was calling anyone else out, how one twenty-year-old contestant wasn't immediately thrown under the bus for being arrogant enough to assume that she deserved to win over contestants who'd been baking for decades. "Just give it a chance," my friend kept saying, tripping balls. "I just love how calming it is, comparatively."

What these shows have in common is their insistence that they are not like other reality TV shows. They aren't trashy—they're deep. They don't roll with the likes of *The Real Housewives* or *America's Next Top Model*. They possess none of the unfiltered mania of old VH1 shows like *Flavor of Love*, *I Love New York*, *A Shot at Love with Tila Tequila*, and Mo'Nique's *Charm School*. They have broken

---

* *The Great British Baking Show*, originally titled *The Great British Bake Off*, was not produced by Netflix, but it was brought to U.S. audiences primarily through their streaming services.

out of the campy unreality of reality TV, instead embracing techniques that, at least superficially, have more in common with documentaries and bad indie films. They try not to call attention to their trashy lineage as they sit at the grown-up table with the likes of the serious TV shows.

More than any of the other networks or platforms, Netflix has promoted its reality television programming as smart, thoughtful, emotionally deep entertainment—barely entertainment at all, really. The preview for *Chef's Table* flaunts the show's Emmy-nominated pedigree ahead of its premise. A handful of episodes of these shows—the fried chicken episode of *Ugly Delicious* and the "Gurki" episode of *Dating Around*, to list just two—have inspired more commentary than most shows are able to generate throughout their entire runs: recaps and interviews and think pieces that analyze their respective cultural importance, each item inflating the show and the episode in the process. My older sister even texted me about the *Ugly Delicious* fried chicken episode and the "intellectual debate" it spawned between her and her husband. Then she made me watch said episode at her house so that I could mediate their argument by, of course, taking her side. As someone who has made a living doing "frivolous" things, like writing, I wondered how important all this really was. After my forced viewing, I got texts from a handful of friends asking, genuinely, if I'd watched the show.

Even some of the Netflix reality TV shows that seem trashy, such as *Nailed It!*, *Awake*, and *Love Is Blind*, are coated in layers of self-awareness, which soften their crudeness and encourage viewers to take them semi-seriously. But the show that looms largest is the genetically modified reboot of *Queer Eye for the Straight Guy*, which over the past few years has handcuffed itself to the mysterious machine that calculates what is and is not culturally relevant. The show has won a handful of Emmys and many more Emmy nominations, generated a barrage of think pieces, and dominated Instagram feeds with heartwarming pictures of its cast members embracing each other's perfect flaws, getting into antics that are supposed to be funny, and being shirtless.

More than any other show in this genre, *Queer Eye* has persuaded audiences that its very existence is deep and meaningful, that we can learn from it and its stars.

TRADITIONAL REALITY TV SHOWS ARE structured around forced spectacles. Whether the show eliminates contestants every week and leans on commercial breaks to drag out every inane dramatic beat, all to build up the hype for a two-hour epic finale, or [is] looser and straightforward, with characters themselves serving as the explosive spectacle, reality television depends on cheap thrills and claustrophobic drama. This is key to both the reality and unreality of the genre. One only has to watch the barrage of catharses that constitute any pre- or post-finale reunion show to understand the methodology.

Queer Eye doesn't operate through forced spectacles. Instead, it seeks to deescalate the intensity of the political issues it raises by suffocating them with thoughtful niceness. The lives of the people the Fab Five encounter aren't in dire need of real intervention or improvement to begin with, unlike, say, the fashion catastrophes one finds on makeover shows. These characters are occasionally messy, but they almost always have loving family members or a wide support network and community. Perhaps they buy unhealthy snacks and clothes from Walmart. Maybe they need help communicating with their loved ones—whether it's a husband who doesn't make enough of an effort during date nights with his wife, going out to nice restaurants in raggedy T-shirts, or a young gay man who feels guilty that he hasn't told his stepmom about his sexuality. But these are not the communication issues one finds on a show like *Hoarders*, whose titular protagonists destroy their physical and personal lives an hour at a time. The characters on *Queer Eye* are basically doing fine. What intensity the show has is a world away from Tyra Banks screaming, "We were all rooting for you!" at Tiffany, a contestant on *America's Next Top Model*'s fourth season, the same season that saw a different contestant undergo an epileptic seizure.

The people featured on *Queer Eye* never become spectacles; their main function is as vessels for sentimental political dialogues that are empty enough to satisfy the expectations of the most banal kind of "wokeness." Contestants talk to the Fab Five about police brutality, homosexuality and the church, and coming out to one's family and community. They learn from these conversations, and we as viewers are supposed to learn, too. Or, if the episode's lesson is already familiar to us, we can simply respond with a beatific smile.

The third episode of *Queer Eye*'s first season, "Dega Don't," opens the way most of the show's episodes do: the Fab Five are driving to their next project, debriefing about the person they will be "more than making over." Sunlight against the windshield submerges the cast in distracting glare. They are meeting Cory, a white thirty-six-year-old police officer who is happily married, though a bit complacent as a husband; he throws NASCAR-themed parties in his basement for his bros. Midway through the drive, we hear police sirens in the background. Tan, Bobby, and Jonathan look back to see what's going on and start cursing. "It's not you guys," Tan says, "it's because they saw me in the background," alluding to his Pakistani ethnicity. The others talk over him, so he is forced to repeat his one-liner, his affect as flat and vapid as the show's high-definition cinematography, in which everything is equally clear and there is no difference between depth and shallowness. "We're getting pulled over," says Karamo, the Fab Five's only Black member and the car's driver, his deadened eyes communicating both annoyance and the sullen resignation that this is indeed his life. At that moment it is hard to tell if Karamo is more frustrated by his upcoming confrontation with the police or [by] his fellow cast members' ham-fisted response to the situation.

Karamo pulls the car over, and a white police officer approaches the driver's-side window. Jonathan begins recording the interaction on his phone, a realistic and necessary response that nonetheless completely upends the reality of the situation, as it prompts the question: Why would they need to record this interaction when, as Bobby points out to the officer, "We're filming a show"? A possible answer: this scene is only masquerading as real life and is, in fact, staged and fictionalized in hopes of teaching the audience how to react in a situation like this, as well as to prove that the Fab Five [are] enlightened enough to know how to react in this situation in the first place.

The officer orders Karamo to get out of the car and begins questioning him about the premise of *Queer Eye*—the scene an inevitable evocation of countless instances of police brutality on Black bodies—before revealing that he's actually friends with Cory, that he was the one who nominated him for the show, and that this is all a big practical joke. The Fab Five shout in relief, and Karamo lunges at the officer, pushing him before they collapse into each other's arms. "You can't do that to brown people," exclaims Tan. "I thought I was going back to Canada," adds Antoni, sounding like a comedian resigned to the fact that his joke is bombing. Everything quickly becomes fine. The tension disperses into a warm hug. But even after the relief of the Fab Five's laughter, it's hard to ignore the fact that Karamo remains a Black man subjected to the whims of the police. The fantasy of the reality TV show cannot conceal this particular reality.

What is this scene's implication? Are we to believe that the Fab Five exudes so much positivity that they can render powerful feelings of trauma—and those oppressive forces that create these feelings—impotent and ineffective? Later in the episode, Karamo is driving Cory to their next destination. The two trade stories from their childhood—how they were raised in similar households, how Cory listened to Wu-Tang Clan and Bone Thugs-n-Harmony. "You and I would've hung out in high school," Karamo says. Only after establishing that the fabulous gay Black man and the white police officer have some overlap in their backgrounds can *Queer Eye* return to the topic of police misconduct and brutality. "The perception right now, especially between Black people and cops, it's tension," Karamo says, nearly drowning his words in thoughtful consideration, exceedingly careful not to trigger Cory or any of the show's white viewers who don't believe they are racist. At this moment, one can be forgiven for thinking that though perpetrator and victim are wildly unequal, on the show, the feelings of both are equally important.

Karamo goes on to say he was "freaking out" when he was pulled over, that he really thought he would be "dragged out of the car," that his own son didn't want to get a license because "he was scared he was gonna get pulled over and get shot by a cop." Right when we think this conversation has finally tapped into the visceral core of the issue at hand, Cory interjects: "I get stereotyped because of that ten percent that gets shown on the media . . . being excessive or killing." After recounting a story of a local cop kicking a handcuffed Black man in the face, Cory laments that "there is nothing that makes it all right." Karamo responds by saying, "Just even hearing you acknowledge that the officer that used force should never have just heals me." The conversation fizzles out into nonsense platitudes. "We're both dealing with the same pain on two different ends," Karamo says—that is, Black people and police officers. "Black Lives Matter," Cory responds, without any real context, before saying "if we could sit and have a conversation . . . things would be a lot better."

In the world of *Queer Eye*, the simple act of sharing stories and listening to others can be weaponized to combat cultural differences, hate crimes, racism, homophobia, and other urgent political issues that occupy the minds of the show's audience. (Throwing money at people in order to improve their looks also helps.) Political healing, in other words, can happen just by having difficult conversations. But even if you accept this premise, none of the political discussions on *Queer Eye* ever builds to a point of catharsis. The conversations remain civil, never shading into spectacle, and as a result, they are ineffective. Arguments are never sustained, points are made only to be counteracted, even if the response isn't apposite. There is no real drama—[not] even the fake kind on trashy reality TV shows.

Spectacle, drama, catharsis—these are the basic narrative strategies that have kept viewers drawn to reality TV since the genre's emergence. You can't stop watching, and in the case of trashy reality TV, you can't stop bearing witness to bad people and bad behavior. Before she was a makeup ad, Lauren Conrad, known back then as LC, wallowed in her self-pitying love for her best friend, Stephen. Episode after episode, I watched her wait on the sidelines of the friend zone for Stephen to break up with his on-and-off-again girlfriend, Kirsten Cavallari, who would later join the cast of *The Hills* and continue to torment our relatable girl next door. For three seasons, *Laguna Beach* forced viewers like me to dwell in its overblown teenage drama. Encountering Conrad's image again—this time highly stylized, the very epitome of femininity, her head thrown back and her lips bright red and plump—I suddenly realized why the first season of *The Hills* placed so much emphasis on her transition from "LC" to "Lauren." Stephen's insistence on calling his best friend LC—and Lauren's acceptance of this—was an effort to de-gender her completely, to rid her of femininity and her viability as a love interest.

Neither *Laguna Beach* nor *The Hills* can be described as

emotionally moving, but this felt more complex, and thus more real, than the strained emotional connections forged on *Queer Eye*. What would have happened if *Queer Eye* had allowed Karamo, or the TV creation of Karamo, to be angrier, to be a spectacle? What if we—particularly queer people of color—were allowed to be justifiably upset, to refuse participation in a dialogue where every voice is heard despite not needing to be? What if, when transgressed and hurt repeatedly, we could escape one world and create a new one, where we would rename ourselves? Maybe then we'd become fashion moguls, our faces plastered onto the side of a Macy's escalator.

—

WRITING ABOUT THE ORIGINAL *Queer Eye for the Straight Guy*, José Esteban Muñoz argues that "the program's weak multiculturalism—namely, its inclusion of one Latino, Jai Rodriguez—is merely a neoliberal injection of a little brownness that is meant to ward off any foreseeable challenges to the overwhelming whiteness that radiates from the increasingly dominant version of queerness." He goes on to agree with Lisa Duggan's account of "neoliberalism's gay agenda." Shows like *Queer Eye*, Duggan writes, create "a demobilized gay constituency and a privatized, depoliticized gay culture anchored in domesticity." It's no accident that the one queer man of color on the old show was reduced to the most inane job—the emotional support hype man who, like Karamo, exists mostly to be, as Judith Butler would say, "merely cultural." The queer brown friend, the designated mediator of civility politics, grants the gay white guys permission to act as though nothing matters but the most consumerist sense of style, as though the neoliberal gay agenda were the answer. "Civility," write Tavia Nyong'o and Kyla Wazana Tompkins, "is the site where the difficulty of articulating class and race together becomes clear." Which is plainly obvious in Karamo's wholly empty—but wholly civil—conversation with Cory in "Dega Don't."

Muñoz wrote his critique of *Queer Eye for the Straight Guy* in 2005, and much of his argument applies to Netflix's revamped version of the show, even as the "injection of a little brownness" has been expanded to a healthy dose of one Black man and one South Asian man. A whole set! But what actually concerns me about *Queer Eye*, what strikes me as novel about the new show, is that the new Fab Five are actually, occasionally—I hate to admit—deep.

In the season 2 premiere—one of the show's most lauded episodes—we see Bobby struggle to set foot into a church, which the Five are making over, because of his fraught history with religion. To the extent that anything on TV can be genuinely moving, this is, in the same way that Karamo's description of his son being afraid to drive is moving, and also in the same way that Jonathan's real-life history is moving, especially when he recounts his experience as a recovering addict, sexual abuse victim, and HIV-positive nonbinary person in his memoir, *Over the Top: A Raw Journey to Self-Love*. Even the Fab Five's foray into Japanese culture and society in [the show's] four-episode special, *Queer Eye: We're in Japan!*, can be read as a sincere attempt to understand social and emotional bonds beyond the American context. But only if you endure the awful, choppy editing that splices conversations between English and Japanese speakers to cut the interpreter out of the scenes, leaving the Fab Five desperately acting as though they understand Japanese and making each interaction feel and look like a bad school video project, one in which all the underachieving students in the group refused to rearrange their schedules to meet, which resulted in all the actors being filmed separately and then one student—probably the only group member who wanted a decent grade—forced to glue everything together. Still, there are moments in this Japan season that are emotionally moving and [of] approximate deepness—when, for instance, the viewer learns about a nurse who invites sick patients to sleep in her home, who has adhered to a Japanese idiom of "giving up on being a woman"—or when you witness the Fab Five at least acknowledge that there is a specific cultural context to being queer in Japan, even if they never really bother to probe that context.

But according to the show's logic, to be moved is to be inevitably displaced farther and farther from reality. Instead, *Queer Eye* encourages us to float away into the deep blinding abyss of pure sentiment, of mantras preaching undeserved self-love ringing in one's ears. The show's confessional scenes seem to beg for this. The background is blurred the way it often is on Skype, as if we're watching the moment through tears, the world—the way it actually appears—impossibly elusive.

If the old guard of reality television appeals to viewers by making them feel better and more enlightened than the vapid, desperate characters on-screen, deep reality TV shows make viewers feel better by establishing and promoting real-life role models whose good deeds are easily mimicked. In order to be a better person, we don't need to win a fierce competition or subject ourselves to an extreme makeover. Instead, we can get a haircut and master one of Antoni's low-effort recipes, like the carrot salad, or a grilled cheese sandwich, or, literally, a grapefruit paired with avocado slices. We can make small adjustments to our lives and change for the better. We can learn to love ourselves. If we do, maybe then the world will become a better place.

This is the world viewers want, or the world Netflix wants on their behalf: a fantasy of society whose characters absolve conflict and morally improve through nice, considerate, ultimately minuscule actions.

In an interview with *GQ* about his show *Maniac*, a boring miniseries starring Emma Stone and Jonah Hill, the director Cary Fukunaga was enthusiastic about Netflix's powers: "Because Netflix is a data company, they know exactly how their viewers watch things," he said. "The algorithm's argument is gonna win at the end of the day." Netflix's implementation of deep learning, or networks that "learn" from large sets of data, has resulted in viewers being targeted with their supposed interests more heavily than ever before. Logging on to Netflix, we are bombarded by genres and thumbnails tailored to us, previews that start playing automatically, recommendation after recommendation after recommendation.

Does deep learning beget deep TV and then deep reality TV? It's true that the beast that is Netflix's algorithm does more than offer recommendations—it dictates aspects of its shows' production, which might explain why shows like *Queer Eye* seem at once overbaked and underdone. Anything that doesn't immediately attract viewers warrants zero effort, no attention to detail. The algorithm knows that there needs to be an emotional conversation every ten minutes, that viewers want to see every tear leaking from each eye socket in detailed HD, even as the color palette of the show can remain stale and bland. The materiality of the Fab Five's makeovers doesn't matter as much as the vague affect of resolution and a job well done. If viewers wanted to see a serious home renovation, rather than a paint job and some flimsy new shelves, they [could] watch something [like] *Property Brothers* or *Extreme Makeover*. If they wanted useful recipes, and not whatever it is Antoni claims he is cooking, they would watch an actual cooking show.

Yet, even as Netflix's all-knowing power burrows deep into our preferences, it is limited: viewership data can't predict the desires that lie beyond our awareness. Netflix's algorithm may know what viewers want *now*, but not what we will want in the future—nor can it accommodate the very human instinct that plagues many of us: the longing for something we don't actually desire.

—

ONE OF THE DEFINING MOMENTS of *Dating Around*—and of deep reality TV as a genre—occurs in the second episode of its first season. This is the aforementioned "Gurki" episode, which inspired two of my best friends from college to send me over thirty texts within the span of fifteen minutes. *Fuck this white guy!!!!!!!!*, the group chat read, before my two friends began commiserating about the depressing state of millennial singledom and how creating a Hinge profile is obnoxiously tedious and labor-intensive.

In the episode, we are introduced to Gurki, a tall and stunning thirty-seven-year-old Indian woman, obviously much cooler than most *Dating Around* protagonists. The dark hues are oversaturated, and the colorful lights scream "romantic night under the stars" like a bad prom theme, as Gurki finds herself on a date with Justin, a twenty-eight-year-old white man. With his dark denim jeans, slick undercut, and full beard, Justin looks like he gets fashion tips from an iPhone app or considers himself a feminist simply because he uses Bumble. (I am convinced Bumble attracts the most toxic of men.) Anyway, Gurki and Justin have what we are meant to think of as deep and meaningful conversations about Justin's previous relationship and Gurki's previous marriage. Gurki explains that her parents met on the day of their arranged marriage, and Justin responds in disbelief. "That's terrible," he says.

Later in the date, they return to the topic of Gurki's marriage, after a previous conversation in which Justin criticized Gurki's doubt-filled decision to marry her ex-husband. They start debating what it means to be in love, and when Gurki calls Justin out for his childish beliefs ("I don't think you've ever been in love"), Justin responds by saying, "How do you know? You got divorced at thirty-two." Then he verbally attacks Gurki, repeating the line "You lied to a man" several times, telling her she "ruined eight years" of her life and her ex-husband's. "How could anyone ever trust you?" he asks.

Frustrated and exhausted, Gurki gives up and lets Justin continue his tantrum. He ends by justifying his own aggressive pedantry: any man she dates would ask her the same questions, tell her the same things, he says, because "you wanna know somebody from their *core*." Everything Justin says in this conversation lands as tone-deaf and downright offensive. He's a date you'd never wish upon anyone. But as Justin himself implies, these are the real romantic interactions that *Dating Around* wants to portray. This is supposed to be reality television at its deepest, rawest, and most real, straight from the inner core of its characters.

And then we get to the end of the episode. In the final minutes, we wait in anticipation to see which of the five men Gurki has picked for a second date. We know she would never, in her right mind, subject herself to another date with Justin, but we still can't help but be nervous. When Gurki appears, she walks down the sidewalk with shopping bags in her hands, and as she wanders off into the distance, we realize she has chosen none of the men. She has chosen herself.

Here *Dating Around* skirts the very edge of filming a dramatic spectacle and then quickly withdraws. Just as Gurki walks off into the sunset with her moral integrity intact, we as viewers are also meant to be moved—emotionally, and almost physically, away from that disastrous date. But while the retreat from outbursts and petty catharsis might spare Gurki from further embarrassment and make audiences feel relieved, it is also the case that nothing bad has happened to Justin, either—he is allowed to walk away from the date, as he literally does in the episode. All we do is leave him behind, which *Dating Around* tries to delude us into thinking is a form of progress.

It isn't. Most viewers know this, as evidenced by the public backlash against Justin and in support of Gurki, which took the form of the usual internet reactions and even an in-depth interview with Gurki herself on Vulture, the epicenter of deep reality TV commentary. What viewers wanted wasn't heartfelt closure but poetic justice. But the occasional longing for something more sharp-edged than fantasy has little power in the battle against the deep reality TV ecosystem. *Dating Around* is the template, and the audience reaction to the Gurki episode the anomaly. Netflix's deep reality offerings don't encourage comeuppance; they project a "woker" world.

And what does this world look like? We can see a glimpse in the "Japan" episode of *The Final Table*, which I was forced to watch by another friend, who pitched it to me as "fucking batshit." This episode, from *The Final Table*'s first season, features our contestants competing to cook the most innovative kaiseki meal, while hewing closely to tradition. The clear front-runner is Darren MacLean, a wide-eyed blond chef who runs a Japanese restaurant in Calgary. Darren spends most of the episode doubling down on his passion for Japanese cuisine. In his confessional interviews, he tells us that he opened his restaurant because he wanted "to share the real Japan with people in Canada," but he needed to study "harder because it doesn't run through [his] veins." He assures audiences that he doesn't want to be "just another white guy trying to make Asian food." He stares so intensely at the camera while speaking that you almost think the producers are holding a gun to his head to make sure he doesn't say anything culturally offensive.

The three Japanese judges compliment his kaiseki dishes, and he thanks them by respectfully bowing. He sprinkles Japanese phrases into everything he says. He's so considerate, so in tune with Japanese culture, that he becomes a walking parody of political correctness. When he and his partner win the challenge, Darren nearly throws his whole body onto the ledge behind him. He bows again. He tears up. The host comments, "I don't think I've seen that much emotion out of you," as Darren tries to give a speech about how deeply grateful he is to win this challenge because, in his words, "I'm not Japanese." In his confessional interview, he even admits, "I haven't felt happy, like super happy, for a while."

Like Antoni's overloaded and calculated performance at Syracuse University, Darren's self-conscious, respectful demeanor becomes so awkward, uncanny, and uncomfortable that you almost wish something bad or offensive had actually taken place. Antoni and Darren's political harmlessness becomes its own kind of torture, offensive in its insistence that nothing is wrong. Throughout the entire episode, Darren completes so many polite gestures and pronounces so many Japanese words correctly and assures the audience that he *knows* he's white so often that he always emerges as inoffensive, though just barely. He is a ticking time bomb, the embodiment of a woker world in which we keep trying to fix a broken system not by restructuring it, but by making sure we never say or do the wrong thing. Yes, Darren never says anything *wrong*, but his desperate attempt to avoid being offensive ends up almost comically laborious, both for him and for the viewers, who have to sit uncomfortably and witness his performance.

Darren's constant self-flagellation keeps him from succumbing, outright and publicly, to his desire for Japanese culture, which then grants him permission from audiences, maybe unintentionally, maybe only in his own mind, to consume Japanese culture even more fully and deeply, to digest it into his very persona, his purpose in life, his primary means of making money. Maybe it's not cultural appropriation, strictly, as Darren isn't ignorant as much as knowledgeable to a fault. But is Darren's self-awareness any better? Maybe it's even worse. I can't help but think that Darren is the type of deep neoliberal person *Queer Eye* is so desperate to create, the type of woke guy that might have won over Gurki, or at least the type of guy that Netflix imagines might win over the Gurkis in its audiences.

Since watching the "Japan" episode together, my friend and I have forced several of our Asian friends to endure the same viewing experience—mostly as a practical joke, but also [as] a call to arms against overzealous stupidity. We've come to the conclusion that watching Darren avoid making a transgression feels as hilariously traumatic as any possible transgression itself would feel. This approach to the maintenance of civility is completely unsustainable. Eventually, someone will trip up the system, and the ruse will explode in our faces. In the meantime, all we can do is wait in utter trepidation, hoping that the world will change because of our meaningless attempts at self-care.

Muñoz and Duggan were worried about *Queer Eye for the Straight Guy*'s work to depoliticize liberal audiences and render them complicit to oppressive privatized capitalism and "overwhelming whiteness." I am worried that *Queer Eye*, and other deep reality TV shows, and "woke" television in general—the *Sex Education*s and *Atypical*s of the world—will nurture a superficial, politicized liberal audience, who will then project weak politics that actually strengthen oppressive systems. But then again, isn't it better that Netflix's algorithm is helping to create deep reality TV and not right-wing trash? Isn't that a good sign? Isn't it noteworthy that the data collected on audiences has revealed a desire for liberal media? Shouldn't we be happy that these TV shows aren't made to embolden radically conservative, even violent audiences?

My thoughts on these questions return to my interactions with my Syracuse students and several arguments I've had with my friends about *Queer Eye*. What I tend to hear is that we need some niceness in our lives, a reprieve from how fucked-up the world is, in order to gather the strength to fight back. And over time, my response has congealed into something like: How can we fight back if we are educated to uphold counterproductive politics? How can we better educate ourselves when our desire for niceness gets in the way? And are niceness and self-care the only ways to allow ourselves a reprieve in the first place?

You can only keep up the precarious act of sustaining this fantasy of a better world for so long when not much has actually changed in our favor. But as long as there's something new in our queue, after binging on a season or two, we can move on, forestalling a confrontation with the shallow, messy world we ultimately inhabit.

PEOU AND HER KMOUYS

FICTION, FROM *STRAIGHT THRU CAMBOTOWN*

All the Great-Mas and Great-Gongs who actually understood Peou, from her youth into her adulthood, from Cambodia to Cambotown, remembered her as having a gift with numbers. Apparently, Peou's mother even thought her a genius, a mathematics prodigy, that she carried so much potential because she memorized the price of each vegetable sold in every Battambang market stall. Then, in the early 1980s, in a land of soda fountains and steel-enforced buildings dedicated to shopping, the Mas of a still-emerging Cambotown found themselves clapping Peou's malnourished cheeks into their hands, their worked-to-death, we-endured-concentration-camps-but-it's-not-as-if-our-previous-lives-had-been-stuffed-with-bliss hands. "If only you were born here, they lamented, you'd be guaranteed a real life. You could be a bank teller, or a store manager, or a cashier on the good side of town. You could be a winner on *The Price Is Right*."

"If only," they chanted. "If only, if only."

But by summer 2014—the time frame for our main saga, this major crossroads in Cambotown history—not even a decade past the Great Recession, Peou was gone. The EMTs found her totaled Mazda too little too late, and the news wrecked the neighborhood (our whole world, really) and then kept rippling, under everyone's homes, echoing into their bones, like the aftershocks of an earthquake. Thinking "if only" felt all the more pointless.

On June 20, 2014, Peou died at fifty-five, after living in the Cambodian neighborhood of Los Angeles County since 1980 (but as a naturalized U.S. citizen since 1992). She left behind two older sisters and two obnoxious brothers-in-law; her three kmouys, already adults; the memory of a husband who'd died in the camps; and no children of her own. From the absolute-zero life given to refugees, she had worked her way up to ruling an empire, to being worth over a million. Though she kept her success quiet and, to those living outside Cambotown, downright invisible.

Yes, when she was alive and breathing, numbers crowded her memory like digital files on a hard drive. But if you ask her kmouys, Peou understood that her gift wasn't so much a facility with numbers as a deeper obsession. Ever since she first started working, laboring, clearing bowls of sloppy noodles as a child at her mother's kuy teav bar in the town market, Peou considered her real talent to be in always knowing, to the finest degree, how much people owed her. Simply put, she held grudges. She was forever tallying up people's offenses to her personhood. And if this talent seemed like a gift with numbers, it was due to her understanding that all numbers were a simple, albeit flawed, system by which people understood and measured how things relate to one another, and wasn't all this measuring of relations itself just an elaborate scheme for figuring out debt? What we owe others. What others owe us. Her habit of memorization, then, stemmed from the conviction that whenever she paid or did more than what she considered fair, she felt owed back the difference, that at one point in the future, everyone in her life would receive their karmic retribution, and their debts to her would at last be paid.

It follows, then—how could it not?—that Peou had assumed the role assigned to brilliant Cambo women and men alike. It was so natural, Peou serving as the Counter. The calculator of interest and debts. The head of her very own Circle of Money, which had sustained the community in the aftermath of history when nothing else could. She managed the numbers that governed Cambotown life. Under her rule, from 1990 to her death, nobody was spared her strict, unforgiving demeanor.

Nobody, that is, but her kmouys: Darren, Vinny, and Molly. To Peou, her two sisters' kids could never do wrong, and if they ever had stumbled into offensive, stupid behaviors, Peou blamed not her kmouys, but her sisters, for being dumb enough, selfish and arrogant enough, to have kids they could barely mother, to have brought lives into this world that had destroyed their culture, their country, their people. This world that had beaten everyone they'd ever known to a fine pulp.

Her kmouys, her beloved kmouys. I'm sure Peou thought of them before she died. In that split second between impact and death, hopefully she wasn't, for once, obsessing over numbers, or debts, or calculated interest. All of that turned irrelevant as her car flipped and hurtled down the 710, everything from the Mazda's windshield to her rib cage shattering into a million pieces. With blood leaking from her skull, with catastrophic pain mangling her body, Peou and her thoughts—I am inclined to imagine—traveled seventeen years into the past. To a memory of her kmouys, which Darren, Vinny, and Molly all mentioned to me offhand, independently of one another, in our conversations about Peou.

This is their memory, as I've envisioned it over the compiling and completion of this text: Her kmouy prohs, Darren and Vinny, are arguing about nonsense in the backseat. In the front and sitting agreeably, Molly, her favorite, her kmouy srei, nods along to an old Cambodian song on the stereo. For context, her kmouys are latchkey kids who never make it home. Their families use a fake address so they can attend the magnet K–8 school in the good district, but it takes an hour, with traffic, to drive to their bus stop from Cambotown. The public library is the only place for them to stay in the afternoons, as their mothers work every overtime shift they can manage, and it is Peou who picks them up when the library closes. But Peou doesn't drive them home, never right away. Instead, she takes them all over Cambotown, through that month's iteration of the Circle of Money.

Darren and Vinny hate that Peou drives them back to their hood, only to drag them to random houses and apartments inhabited by other Mings and Pous they barely know, other Mas and Gongs and Bongs. But Molly loves watching

Peou demand money from people. In Molly's eyes, Peou is the red-hot center of Cambotown. As the only kmouy who bothers to ask about Peou's job, Molly has learned all the mechanics of the Circle of Money her nine-year-old brain can possibly understand. She understands that participating Cambos contribute money into a communal pot. She understands that contributors are entitled to interest based on the size of their contributions and that every month, a different contributor can take their "turn" and borrow money from the communal pot, provided that they pay back the full amount, plus interest. She even understands that Peou collects everyone's owed amount, regardless of how long it takes, how difficult some Cambos end up being; and then, after taking her cut, Peou redistributes this collected interest to each contributor. Although Molly doesn't yet understand the meaning of "interest."

Usually, in these car rides, Peou finds herself lecturing her kmouys, talking their ears off. About what? Anything: The welfare state, Cambo gangs, why some snobby Cambos are in denial about being Cambodian and call themselves Chinese, the absurdity of cow's milk, how condensed milk is just poison the French used to cripple the lactose-intolerant peoples of Indochina, how they all need to be good with money, how all stores in the U.S. should have a bartering system in place because fixed prices will be the death of the economy—because what is communism other than a fixed-price equalizing society?—how her sisters are well meaning, yes, and while her kmouys should always respect their elders, they really shouldn't take what their mothers say that seriously.

Peou talks because she wants to be a good role model, to impart some wisdom onto her kmouys, to warn them of what the harsh world has in store for them, to shed a light on what their mothers don't understand, let alone teach, and also because she's not about to smoke in front of her kmouys. So, she needs to do something with herself.

But in this moment, Peou isn't ranting for her kmouys to trust nobody with their hard-earned money, not even their loved ones, or for them to choose their future professions with care, since the world might look completely different in thirty years, since even engineers or lawyers or doctors can become obsolete in the wake of a political coup. Today, she has barely spoken since picking up Darren, Vinny, and Molly from the library. For once, she doesn't even feel the urge to smoke a cigarette. She is at peace, almost.

Maybe she feels this way because she has just reconnected with her brother-in-law Vithara, which has proved more than a little useful. His investments have expanded her Circle of Money tenfold, cementing her financial security for the future to come. The sudden appearance of Vithara—years after his vanishing, right before the fall of Pol Pot—has made her happy on a number of levels. His resemblance to his older brother, for one, has helped her recollect details about her dead husband. With Vithara as her business partner, she remembers her husband's stringy hair flopping onto his face, those shoulders of his that struck her as unreasonably broad, that smirk he gave in response to her affection, as if she were forbidden territory he had snuck into and settled anyway. Or maybe it's simpler than that. Maybe she's enjoying the song on the stereo, the early touches of autumn creeping into the dry heat, and her kmouys riding along with her on this drive through Cambotown. Unfortunately, these moments can always be ruptured.

In the backseat, Darren and Vinny's argument has escalated into a slap fight, and upon getting slapped right in the eye, Darren yells, "Fuck!"

"Watch your mouth!" Peou says. "Want me to sell you at the market?"

Darren and Vinny immediately stop fighting, and the only sounds in the car now come from the stereo. A slow, romantic song from the golden age of Cambodia, before all that political upheaval. A male tenor singing the highest notes he can, his falsetto warbling each word to blur into the next. Musicians plucking khims, erhus, and tros, their staccato notes echoing the backup singers, who whistle cascading trills like chimes in the wind, layering honeyed sadness onto the main singer's smooth cooing.

After the song ends, Molly points at the stereo. She asks, "Ming, what was that about?"

Peou, to her own surprise, draws a blank. She presses Rewind to replay the song, concentrates on the lyrics anew, but every time she's about to grasp some meaning, she fails. The singer evades her understanding with an abrupt change in key. A static buzz muffles the articulation. The instrumentals overpower the words.

She wonders if her Khmer is now faltering due to a decade of switching to and from English. Or maybe the shoddy tape—a bootleg of a bootleg of an artifact—had been corrupted. After all, she reasons, these tapes were sold in the park, by Mas on welfare peddling up-charged souvenirs from the homeland. Still, the thought of losing her mother tongue rumbles in her mind.

"Earth to Ming," Molly says, "What's the singer singing about, anyway?"

"Yeah, we wanna know," Vinny whines from the back.

"I don't know," Peou says softly, focusing on the road.

"But it's in Khmer," Darren says.

"You think I don't know that?" Peou snaps, and everyone quiets. Peou merges onto Anaheim Street, which hundreds of commuters take to avoid traffic when driving from their Orange County homes to their Los Angeles jobs, barely aware of the largest community of Cambodian Americans in the country. Darren, Vinny, and Molly look disturbed, Peou notices before turning off the stereo.

"Tape's no good," Peou says.

"But . . . that's so sad," Molly responds.

"You mean we won't ever understand the lyrics?" Vinny asks.

"No, I'm not saying that," Peou says. Then a breath, another pause. "But you know, some things are just lost. So, don't waste your life thinking about it."

Her kmouys soak in her words, and she hopes it's for the best. The remainder of their drive, Peou craves the harshness of hand-rolled cigarettes, that nicotine buzz, the taste of ash and lighter fluid always alleviating the grueling asceticism practiced by the Buddhist monks. She swallows instead her unyielding impulse to smoke. Her kmouys, her beloved kmouys. Their lungs still inhale and hold the air they need. That capacity for breath, life itself, she refuses to compromise.

DARREN AND VINNY

FICTION, FROM *STRAIGHT THRU CAMBOTOWN*

Three days after Peou's death, as he rode to Oakland for his cousin's concert, Darren found himself remembering a wisecrack he'd said to Vinny around ten years before. The memory right then was so vivid and real, he told me during our first of many conversations. His subconscious had conjured it despite that metallic roar of the BART.

The night of the wisecrack was Darren's eighteenth birthday, and of course Vinny and him were at Little Caesars, splitting a five-dollar pizza and two-dollar garlic sticks. Finally, both of them had made it, they were goddamn adults. They could splurge on lottery tickets. And cigarettes! They possessed the power to vote and sway elections and now, hypothetically, choose how they lived their lives.

"What's really wild," Darren said, slathering hoisin sauce and chili oil onto his slice, "totally more wild than turning eighteen, is how Cambo prohs start middle school, and then, all of a sudden, they're in fucking crisis mode, you know, 'cause they gotta decide whether they're gonna be Yellow or Brown."

Vinny spit out his drink, drenching his plate, and cracked up.

"Fucking shit, Vinny," Darren said. "It's bad enough you drink Code Red Mountain Dew like an obese ten-year-old."

"Sorry man, but damn, that's some real talk," Vinny said. "Real like these dope sauces you brought." He flicked his wrists, pointed at the swirls of dark red hoisin, and slapped his stomach with both hands. "Best pizza I've had."

At the time, Darren thought of comedy as philosophy. No matter how flippant, jokes had the potential of feeling cosmically true, as if the whole universe were to align and cohere when refracted through far-fetched premises, all skewed with enough absurdity to convey real clarity, ideas never before thought, radical understandings of the world. That zinger he told on his eighteenth birthday was no different (though hardly a joke). He really did see an ethical, spiritual, potentially existential, and even ancestral dilemma in the way Cambo prohs were forced to decide on championing string quartets or Wu-Tang listening parties, to live either as mainstream Asian nerds or wannabe, off-brand gangsters. Generations of the tightest cliques of young Cambo prohs, time and time again, reached breaking points once the first pimples had emerged from the epidermal surface of those baby-cheeked faces. Upon entering high school, some Cambo prohs would arm themselves with colossal backpacks stuffed and rolling with textbooks on tiny wheels, while other prohs would sport wifebeaters and jeans that draped over their asses. They spent their weekends spinning donuts in empty lots, car seats reeking of skunk, finished joints littering the concrete, as their counterparts were chugging Red Bulls and snorting Adderall at study parties, cramming SAT and AP vocabulary terms into their swollen brains.

Repping Khmai was off the table, straight up, Darren ranted to Vinny with a mouth full of dough, marinara, Italian seasoning. No, you're required to identify as Yellow or Brown. "Assimilated into the whites" or "the Black people of Asians," if you wanted to be hardcore (and ignorant). It was the simplest form of survival in the U.S., of dealing with the burden of Khmer ancestry, of living in the aftermath of a genocide no one else remembered, let alone bothered to learn about. Unless, of course, you wanted a hellish eternity of explaining the history of Cambodia, and most likely its literal location, to dumbass people.

Whenever he struck gold with a great punch line, Darren saw himself as a genius, his every glib observation providing crucial evidence of a groundbreaking theory, and he felt seriously brilliant that night when he realized, while sitting in Vinny's car with Little Caesars' acid reflux, high out of his mind on a birthday joint, that Cambotown's surrounding urban geography corroborated his joke on the moral, Yellow/Brown dilemma plaguing young and restless prohs.

Cambotown, after all, sat under South Los Angeles and Compton, flanked on either side by Torrance and Westminster. Hardly any Cambo children of refugees ever dreamed of staying in their hometown, stuck without career prospects inside that five-by-five grid of donut shops, jewelry stores, DVD stores loaning out karaoke videos from the homeland, but then the question presented itself: Should Cambo prohs face north, toward the Latino and Black populations of Compton, and affiliate themselves with the subversive ethos of rappers like N.W.A.? Or was it better to charge outward in lateral directions? West for the humble Korean and Japanese enclaves of Torrance. East if the solution was to sell your soul to corporate America and burrow deeper into assimilation, passing through Westminster (that haven of dim sum restaurants) until you hit the OC mansions, Irvine's model minority suburbs, that median household income of $90K a year.

Darren was reminded of this old wisecrack of his, nearly a decade after its first utterance, as he contemplated Vinny's own very funny philosophy of life. Apparently, the answer to the world's most crippling systemic problems, Darren had recently learned, this new philosophy upheld one life motto, a single and resolute tenet: society was in dire need of good Cambo dick. Specifically, Vinny's Cambo dick. Which was a fine piece of machinery, supposedly, as ten thousand YouTube viewers (and now a semi-repulsed Darren) had come to know by listening to the underground rapper's biggest hit to date.

All afternoon, while skimming humorless texts on the theory of comedy in the dusty stacks of Stanford's library, Darren had played Vinny's song on repeat, his ears ringing with the Auto-Tuned voices of the Khmai Kong Rappers. Half-sung raps laid over an uproarious beat of steel drum rhythms and background vocalists shouting good-vibe chants, it was as though the god of verbose swagger had miraculously fused with the god of cheeky energy, only for Vinny to crank up the tempo and volume through an unbroken, manic crescendo lasting a whopping six minutes and twenty-four seconds. Darren had to admit: "Sachkrok Thom," or "Big Sausage," fucking blew his mind.

Sweating on the red Richmond Line, under a hundred feet of ocean via the Transbay Tube, Darren found himself still listening to "Sachkrok Thom," still thinking of that joke from his eighteenth birthday. The year was now 2014, three decades after the first Cambo refugees had settled in California, and here was Darren at the age of twenty-eight, completely unable to pinpoint how his experiences had produced the man he'd become. A goatee on his chin to prove he could grow facial hair, he wore tortoiseshell eyeglasses and Oxford shirts. His medium-length black hair, which he gelled and parted and slicked into unnatural waves, gave him the look of being in perpetual attendance of an élitist networking event, the kind catered with seasonal IPAs and tiny quiches. Which was his world now, really, wasn't it? A PhD student at some bullshit prestigious university, he studied the philosophy of comedy in a bullshit department called Modern Thought and Literature.

On one hand, he was proud of his accomplishments, had figured he was Stanford's only Cambodian PhD student in the humanities. But on the other . . . how the hell did he get so damn white? Yes, everyone felt it, his friends and family had discerned it, how far removed Darren stood from all those years of shitty open mics, from his early twenties of flannel shirts and backward-turned hats, when he opened two-minute comedy sets in the Tenderloin by shouting:

"Hello, hello, I'm Darren, that is my name, and I'm Cambodian! So, you're welcome, now you know a Cambodian guy! You can cross that off your fucked-up list of obscure ethnicities you're trying to meet, you monsters, because, like, I know you guys are always playing racial bingo or whatever behind our backs, trying to make like Pokémon and collect them all. But seriously, being Cambodian is . . . weird. Like, I'm off-brand Asian, you know? I have less in common with mainstream Asians, like Chinese, Japanese, the usual suspects, than, say, middle-aged Jewish people, because—and let me be real with you for a second before I start talking boners or some shit—both older Jewish folks and young Cambos have parents who either survived or died in a genocide!"

And then there was Vinny. Darren's cousin was the first Cambo rapper to break into the hip-hop scene. With tattoos traversing his chest and crawling up his neck, with that rolled-up bandanna always tied around his forehead even though he kept his head shaved, he spit out rhymes about his supposedly impressive dick like he was the second coming of the Ying Yang Twins in "Wait (The Whisper Song)." Maybe this was why the two cousins had grown apart over the past two years, to the point that Darren hadn't even known Vinny was recording a new song. Ten years after graduating high school, Darren and Vinny had assimilated to opposite sides of the Cambo proh racial complex spectrum.

His train emerged out of the water and charged into West Oakland, and Darren felt relieved to see a flash of purple-orange sky, those docks that looked obsolete. It always shot his nerves, the BART, with its permanent stench of the homeless and tech workers steeped in Axe deodorant, with its gray-blue seating that depressed everyone. Whenever he rode to Oakland, he had to reassure himself: the people in the Transbay Tube, at the bottom of the Bay, they were the safest—they really were!—from the big 1989 Loma Prieta earthquake. So, he hardly visited Oakland.

He looked around at the other passengers, half-hoping to find, in the reflections lurking in the windows, in the faces of middle-aged Asian women, an image of his Ming Peou. A dull pang throbbed in his chest. Heaviness slid over his eyes. All he had left of her were his shoddy memories.

Had Darren stopped bullshitting, stopped being his avoidant self, had he shed those defensive layers of self-deprecation and philosophical musings, he would admit to a deeper reason for his obsession with Vinny's new song. He would have accepted that, listening to "Sachkrok Thom," he felt a mix of guilt, pride, aversion, enthusiasm, and, yes, envy. Guilt for the fact that, after Vinny moved to Oakland three months ago to finish recording his album with a local sound mixer, Darren hadn't found the time to visit him until now. Pride because he was genuinely happy that his cousin had achieved this professional breakthrough. Aversion because he probably didn't need to be listening to his cousin rap, on repeat, about his dick. Enthusiasm because the song was catchy, energetic, and upbeat, one of those bangers that compelled you to dance and shout chorus lines and ride the wave of its musical crescendo. And envy because the lyrics were funny, as unabashedly absurd and appealing and clever as Vinny himself. They were funnier than anything Darren had written in the past year.

But mostly, Darren felt confused. He spent the better part

of his afternoon trying to interpret a certain stanza of Vinny's lyrics:

> My dick's reincarnated dick,
> I fuck with a millennium of experience, bitch
> But I humble, I promise
> Don't discriminate, a pussy, an ass
> Don't worry if it's a g-spot or prostate I'm hittin
> Y'all should be at my sachkrok thom's biddin.

Was his cousin, his best friend, coming out? And if so, why in a song? Was his music the only way he could be vulnerable with the world? Even with the one person in their family, their whole community, who would understand, Darren himself having been out as gay since George W. Bush's first presidential term? Since before 9/11!

Darren got off the BART at 19th Street and started walking over to the club where Vinny was headlining. He carried a backpack stuffed with his laptop, some clothes and toiletries, a few philosophy books from the library. The plan was to catch a ride with Vinny downstate to Cambotown. Peou's funeral was in two days.

He arrived at the club an hour before the concert. It was that point of late spring when the nights still dropped to a bone-chilling cold, the ocean breeze amplified by the desert air of the drought. People were loitering outside, smoking cigarettes or puffing their vapes. A short line ran from the edge of the building to the box office, which stood underneath a marquee backlit by the haze of the setting sun. Black letters advertised the Khmai Kong Rappers.

Blasting from his earbuds and into his ear canals, tunneling into the neurons of his brain, the material of his memories, "Sachkrok Thom" played again for what felt like the thousandth time, and Darren joined the line. He wondered how inappropriate it was to be standing here, in the wake of Peou's death, at the very adult age of twenty-eight, speculating about where his cousin happened to be inserting his dick. Then he laughed to himself.

—

ACCORDING TO THE LYRICS OF "Sachkrok Thom," a decent Cambo dick could solve the housing crisis; the decade-long drought and climate change; the gentrification of San Francisco and Oakland and Los Angeles; the rising popularity of Thai food when it was just a too-sweet, rip-off version of Khmer food; the fact that elementary schools had stopped teaching the rules of grammar and cursive; and the impending earthquake along the San Andreas Fault that would send every California resident straight into the ocean. The reasoning, as far as Darren could tell, was that if America could get over its marginalization of Asian (particularly Southeast Asian) dick, it might learn to address its other issues.

Darren sat at the bar nursing a Heineken (the only beer he'd ever seen Cambos drink), as though this beer alone could spiritually transition him back into Cambotown from his Stanford life. He thought about Vinny's reaction to his own coming out, back when they were sixteen and angsty and hopeful. It happened in 2001, and they had hot-boxed Vinny's gold 1990 Corolla while listening to a burned copy of "I Am . . ." by Nas. Back and forth they passed a poorly rolled joint, weed grown by their second cousins' Gong. Vinny was talking about his latest hookup—a Korean girl from his Geometry class, who forced Vinny to climb the fire escape of her parents' apartment building, a full five stories, to enter her bedroom.

"It's bullshit, man," Vinny said. "She doesn't want her parents to know she's with a Cambo. You know, a Brown Asian. Trash or some shit."

He went on to describe in detail the last sexual encounter they had, before Darren interrupted him and said, "I'm too high for this."

"Why, you gay now or something?" Vinny joked.

And Darren, without meaning to, said, "Yeah, I am."

Between the two cousins, a silence pressed itself into the rhythm of the music.

"Wait, you serious?" And then hesitation, a reckoning of what was true, and Darren nodding his head slowly up and down.

"Shit," Vinny said, sinking into the driver's seat. He placed his hands on the steering wheel, like they had anywhere to be but this parking lot of a Dollar Tree store. "Too bad you're not white."

Darren scrunched his face. "What the fuck are you saying?"

"Dude," Vinny answered, "the only people who care about gay guys are white people. They eat that shit up. You know? All those parades. That's some white shit. Everyone else, well . . . you're shit out of luck."

"Fuck," Darren said, before the cousins began to crack up, smothering their previous silence with laughter. And as long as they kept laughing, they felt that everything, maybe, would be all right.

This laughter would buoy them, again and again, through their time in high school and even after Darren went off to UC Berkeley and Vinny stayed in Cambotown to jumpstart his rapping career, but then with less frequency as they reached the age at which you need to be careful about decisions, as, with adulthood, whether you realize it or not, decisions take root and spread and sprout into life. And now, living a bridge away from one another, you'd think this laughter would return to them, in full force, that it'd ring beyond their memories and manifest into an easy reunion. Yes, you would think.

Darren scanned the club again. The crowd was filled with white hipsters, all of them flaunting fringe bangs or trimmed beards, denim jackets on raw denim jeans, piercings glimmering out on the dance floor. They flocked to Vinny as though he were a cult leader, as though, in chanting, "We all motherfucking Cambos," they could forget their own sheltered histories, become indoctrinated into some new world order.

He finished his beer and ordered a second, his cheeks flushed with the patchy glow he would mock in himself during stand-up sets. The concert was about to start, the venue's staff sweeping unnecessary equipment off the stage. The main lights dimmed so that the lines demarcating one body from the next softened and blurred into grainy shadows. The room smelled of stale sweat and the sour tart of old alcohol rotting into resin.

A bearded man in a colorful Hawaiian shirt, the design a collage of parrots, approached the bar. He leaned against the counter and ordered a drink. When he paid the bartender, his arm grazed Darren's back, and Darren's "Asian glow" burned even hotter. Darren bumped into the man's body, slightly, but enough for the man to place his hands on Darren's back in response. Darren caught a whiff of him—cigarette smoke and lavender body wash.

"Sorry," Darren said, turning around, "I have zero body awareness. Also, I'm a dumb fuck." He grinned and raised his eyebrows in tandem with his shoulders.

"Not a problem here," the man said. He took a drink of his beer, then sat down next to Darren. "I'm fucking pumped for this show."

"So, you're, like, a major fan?"

"I just think the Khmai Kong Rappers are—I've just never seen anything like 'em."

"You mean you've never seen a Cambodian rapper, or you've never seen a Cambodian guy?"

"Yeah, totally—I mean—wait." He started to blush, spilled some of his drink. "I mean, I've been . . . actually, to Cambodia!"

"Uh-huh, right."

"Have you been?" The man was getting excited. "Seriously. You should go. God, I wanna just quit my life and go back. And what happened to that country—my fucking god, I still can't believe it. That's why I think Khmai Kong is so good, you know? It's just so meaningful for these guys to be up here rapping their truths."

Darren shot him a quizzical look, a what-the-fuck-are-you-saying-right-now expression from the furrow of his eyebrows to the clenching of his jaw, but the guy didn't notice, so intently did he believe his own words. He was tall and pudgy, in an athletic way, with ample chest hair peeking out from his partially unbuttoned shirt. Darren wanted to straddle him and feel that body hair tickle his inner thighs. He wanted the man to pin him down and thrust into him. But only if he'd shut the fuck up about Cambodia.

"You should talk to Vinny after the show. You know, make a move. He's pretty cute for a Cambodian rapper."

"Yeah, I don't think that would work," the man said, letting out a dry laugh.

Darren leaned closer. "What do you think of the new song?"

"Oh, it's fucking genius. Not to mention hilarious. And just—I don't know—so damn radical."

"What else, though?" Darren took another sip of his beer. "Don't you think, like, there's a new personal dimension he's exploring now, maybe, in his lyrics . . ."

"Well, the political is always personal, right?"

Darren slammed his drink onto the counter. Suddenly it felt unbearable to keep talking to this clown. This happened to Darren, with men, with academic interests—hell, with just about everything. A crossed line, an epiphany, the flip of a switch. Darren always knew exactly what he wanted until he very much didn't.

Avoiding eye contact with the man, he searched for his next words, started strategizing escape routes from their conversation, but then the pre-concert music stopped playing. "Anyway, nice talking to you," the man said, drifting back into the crowd. Relieved, Darren swiveled his barstool around.

Spotlights beamed red and blue onto the stage, the colors mixing into a deep fuchsia, as synthesizers reverberated a steady rhythm. After a moment, Vinny, shirtless and repping his requisite folded bandanna, his tattoos nearly glowing, stepped into the light. One hand beating his chest, the other carrying a microphone while fist-pumping the air, he shouted, "Jom reab suar, Oakland!"

The room responded with an ear-splitting roar, as the synthesizers increased in volume, the two sounds merging together and turning synonymous with the muggy air. The other Khmai Kong Rappers, Kelvin and Rithy, friends of theirs from childhood, spiraled around Vinny, bookending his slender frame with their bulk, chanting, "What up—what up—what up—what up—what up—EAAASSSSSSTT BAAAAAAAAAAAY."

Vinny brought the mic to his face. "Let's get this party started, my bong sreis and prohs!" he yelled, and as the first beat dropped, Darren braced himself.

—

OUT OF EVERYONE HE KNEW growing up in Cambotown, Darren had considered himself the only Cambo proh who could actually sidestep the Cambo proh racial complex. For one, his gayness rendered him immune (mostly) to the pressures of proving his masculine worth. Unlike his peers, he never felt the need to measure his dick size before "fucking bitches"; nor did he ever get scammed into thinking, by some chauvinistic Pou, that an astronomical net worth would make the war and genocide almost seem worth it. (As in: Without Pol Pot, without Kissinger bombing Cambodia, and without all those other tragedies that made the world pity them, wouldn't Cambos be trapped in the poverty of the homeland?)

But mainly, Darren had always been the exception, especially after his father bailed on him and his mom. The smartest kid in his classes, even when compared to the white kids with generational wealth or to the mainstream Asians whose parents had PhDs from both their native countries and an American university, he had gotten into UC Berkeley without breaking a sweat. He had even fallen asleep during the last twenty minutes of the SATs, leaving an entire page blank, and still received a near-perfect score. At just under six foot, he was taller than every Cambo proh in town, other than his second cousin Kenny, who, since hitting puberty, had ruined every family photo. (After graduating high school, Kenny joined the army, then had a brief stint as an MMA fighter before quitting to pursue his dream of owning a "quaint and elegant café" that sold coffee in plastic bags, like in the markets of Phnom Penh.) And then there were Darren's looks. Every Ma in Cambotown raved about how handsome he was. Clearly, his sexuality was irrelevant when it came to setting him up with their granddaughters. "Why waste all of that?" they scolded, running into him at the grocery store or in the park or while ordering a decaf latte in a plastic bag at Kenny's café. What's the point of this facial structure, all these smarts, being this good a son?

Yes, what was the point? What nobody told Darren about being the exception, the success story, was how boring everything got in that final percentile. By the time he started college, he had felt his life becoming ... frictionless. It didn't help that his mother, known by everyone in Cambotown as Ming Nary, had never once adopted an optimistic worldview when parenting. ("The world is bad," Ming Nary would say after complaining about her boss at the DMV. "How do I keep finding myself under oppressive dictators?")

Since he was a teenager, Darren often envisioned himself as full of hot, empty air, like one of those inflatable dancing tubes in front of car dealerships, but shaped like a Cambo proh and untethered from its base. Without exerting much effort, he would gently rise into the sky. He would feel, for a while, the rush of that upward mobility, like the tickle he had felt in his groin as a kid at the park, when kicking himself up on the swings, higher and higher. But then he would feel uneasy. Looking down, he'd see how small everything was, how pointless. What he wanted in moments like this—long after he'd left that playground, after the perfect grades, the Berkeley diploma—was for someone to prick a needle into him, release all that hot air, so that he could crash down to the ground and feel anything but that floating into nothing.

It was the thing that had driven him to comedy, when he stopped to think about it, this uncanny sensation of futile ascent. In comedy, the inescapable pointlessness of it all—that was the point. Irreverence equaled success. Being serious was death. Subjectivity became unavoidable, as anyone could deem something funny or (crushingly) not. There was always someone refusing to laugh, dragging Darren back down to reality, forcing him to refine a punch line, to improvise a new tangent, and he loved that feeling of winning over a resistant audience. Comedy kept Darren grounded, allowed him to feel normal.

But then, even jokes started to bore him. Or, rather, the struggle of keeping one's life afloat while pursuing stand-up comedy. For three years after he graduated college, Darren worked a mindless data entry job and tutored rich kids, just to afford his life of hitting every open mic and bringer show he could. He wasn't unsuccessful in his stand-up career, either. He booked decent shows in the Tenderloin, was a regular performer at the Punchline. But none of it equaled money, paychecks, a livable wage. So, when his former Philosophy professor suggested he apply to graduate school, recommending he study under a Stanford professor with his exact interests—the philosophy of comedy—and when he got into Stanford and was offered a $35K yearly stipend with health care, of course he packed up his Berkeley apartment and moved to the heart of Silicon Valley.

Now he was getting paid to attend school, which had always been a breeze for Darren. And, look, sure—he loved both philosophy and comedy. So, this was a dream come true, he told himself, while zoning out during his weekly seminars, or while reading Kant's incongruity theory of humor or Freud's relief theory of laughter, to realize, after skimming hundreds of pages, he had retained precisely none of it.

"Y'all ready for this next one?" Vinny asked the crowd, as Kelvin and Rithy skipped along the edge of the stage, hyping the crowd for the biggest song of the night, the bass still booming. The ceiling lights shut off, and the room plunged into blackness. A deep red hue began to illuminate the stage. The Khmai Kong Rappers looked menacing yet protective as they regrouped into formation.

The opening of "Sachkrok Thom" blared from the speakers, the crowd hollering in response. Everyone started dancing, rocking their hips back and forth, bouncing their shoulders to the beat. As Vinny launched into the song's lyrics, Darren wondered if anyone else had caught the same potential reveal of sexual preference. He was sure that no one followed Vinny's music as closely as he did, but . . . it was pretty obvious, right?

The song was almost at its critical stanza. Darren followed his cousin's every dance move, each head bop and side step, listened to the dips and turns of his voice. He tried looking deeper into his cousin's face. What he was looking for exactly, he didn't know. A quiver of truth in Vinny's lips? A look of relief in his expression? He kept trying and trying, as though he should be able to know, just know, anything about his cousin by studying his image. Especially this.

But Vinny was too far away to be seen clearly, and the live version of "Sachkrok Thom" sounded the same, more or less, as the recorded one. Nothing seemed that different about Vinny. He was simply in the zone, reciting lyrics at the speed of light. Each cadence he hit with a different register in his voice. Each line was a sonic experience. For the entire song, Vinny remained in total control, complete ownership, of himself.

—

WHEN THE CONCERT WAS OVER, Darren texted Vinny to meet at the bar. The crowd cleared out of the room, and the staff began picking up the leftover trash. As Darren sipped another Heineken, Vinny strolled up from behind and pounced on him, flinging his weight onto his cousin's shoulders.

Darren spit up his drink over the bar. "Dude, the fuck?"

"The fuck yourself, with this IT garb." Vinny popped his head to the side to give his cousin a full look. "This what the gays into now?"

Darren rolled his eyes, stood up, and the cousins fell into an embrace, stayed in each other's arms and started rocking back and forth. Then they separated and sat down. Vinny ordered a Coke and rum, and Darren examined his cousin's face. Why would he say that, Darren wondered, that thing about gay guys?

"You gotta chill," Vinny said, before sipping his drink.

Darren furrowed his eyebrows. "What?"

"You're lost right now." Vinny pointed into his cousin's face, right between his eyes. "I can see it," he added, before spreading his arms open to encompass the room. "You're not here."

Darren broke free from his own staring. "What're you talking about?"

"Ming Peou, man. What do you think?"

"Oh. Right."

"She's gone, but you know, like, what is 'being gone'? 'Cause, she's not gone gone, man. She'll never be."

"Yeah," Darren said. "She's too crazy to ever stop caring about us. We'll be, like, at the bank or some shit, and she'll be reincarnated as the bank teller, shitting on us for fucking with CDs when we should be investing in real shit."

He laughed, and then Vinny laughed, and for a moment,

their laughter inflated them with good vibes. Then, a sinking feeling, from their chests down to their stomachs.

"Wait," Vinny said, "what do you think's happening with Ming Peou's stuff?"

"I haven't thought about it," Darren said.

"Don't be dense, man," Vinny said. "We gotta prepare for shit to get ugly. Me, you, Molly, we gotta band together, make sure we get what we deserve, split that shit evenly."

"I mean, we don't even know if there's a will," Darren said. "Plus, Molly's definitely gonna get everything. If there is money or shit to get."

"Bruh, of course there's money!" Vinny said. "And we're, like, all Ming Peou's favorites, so Molly's not gonna get it all. I bet some of that old jewelry—"

"That's not true," Darren said. "Ming Peou definitely loved Molly more than us. Also, Molly needs the money."

Vinny blinked his eyes, rapidly and repeatedly, like he was trying to unsee something. "You don't know shit," he said, "about which of us needs money the most, and Molly's the one who decided to fuck off in New York and bury herself in debt. She doesn't deserve more because she went to college."

Darren looked down at his bottle, rubbed his thumb against the beer label. "Sorry," he said, fraying damp paper.

"She was hard on us 'cause we're men." Vinny took a breath, then finished his drink in one go. "Not because she loved Molly more." He dropped his glass onto the counter.

Darren flinched at the sound, a loud thud startling the air, and wondered what Vinny's endgame was for this conversation. Though he knew there was no point in rationalizing

Vinny's thoughts, even without the grieving aspect, and, anyway, it did make sense to be curious about the money, right? "Has your mom said anything about a will?"

"Nah. Yours?"

Darren shook his head.

A couple of drinks later, Darren and Vinny were steeped in a silence that was, for the most part, comfortable. They had talked about their plans for the next day, the gas station snacks they would buy for the six-hour drive home. They talked about Molly being stuck living at home again.

As Darren finished his sixth drink of the night, he was on the verge of asking Vinny straight up, to confront him about his apparent "coming out," but tried a different tack. "Dude," he said, "this song came out of nowhere—it's fucking killer."

"It just poured outta me, you know," Vinny said, before taking a deep breath. He closed his eyes. "I got the music flowing out my veins these days."

"It would've been nice, though, to know you were writing new stuff."

And Vinny made a face, a what-the-fuck-you-tryna-ask-me-right-now look. "Yeah, well, you're busy with shit."

"What's that supposed to mean?"

"Nothing. Seriously, I don't mean a thing." Now Vinny shook his head. "How's Staaaannnnnnnfooooooorrrrrrd?"

"Oh, you know—same old, same old," Darren answered, ignoring Vinny's tone. "The rich guy circle jerk, still as prestigious as ever." He grinned to make sure Vinny knew he was joking.

"Yeah? And what else? That all you gonna tell me?"

Darren opened his mouth and said nothing. He was

confused by Vinny's mild aggression. Vinny was the kind of guy who told strangers he loved them at parties, held their faces in his hands, peering into their eyes for hopeful glimpses of the future, after sharing with them a joint he'd rolled himself. Vinny, in Darren's mind, had always been a good guy, obnoxiously so.

"I don't know," Darren said. "I guess I'm kind of sick of it, you know? My professors, my cohort, the fact that I say 'cohort' now. Everyone's on this high horse about themselves. None of the other grad students get the difference between being poor—like, *actually* poor—and being broke. They're all rich kids ashamed of being rich. And so, they preach Marxist nonsense about how Stanford treats them as unpaid labor and shit, and I'm like, dude, you chose this life. You weren't some manufactured cultural type. You literally applied to become a grad student. This guy from my cohort, like, he legit said the other day that we were all 'living in poverty.' Meanwhile, his parents are fucking lawyers. Meanwhile, he doesn't know shpat about the income cutoff for poverty. I'm over grad students victimizing themselves and shit. You can make more money working full time at Starbucks, so why not just do that?"

"Fucking shit, bruh," Vinny said, eyes glazed over. "When did you get so negative?"

"You asked," Darren said, steadying himself on the stool. He felt driven back by his cousin's energy.

"What're you even doing these days?" Vinny pressed.

"I told you—working on my dissertation proposal."

"You say that like it's important."

"Jesus, tell me how you really feel."

"It's just—what happened to our pact?" Vinny said. "What happened to doing something legit with our lives? When's the last time you even performed some actual jokes?"

Vinny's sentiments had hit Darren right in the face. What had he said to trigger his cousin? But Vinny had angered him, too. He was doing the thing. He was still doing comedy. Just in a different . . . venue.

"Let's just fucking, like, stop," Darren said. "I'm not in the mood."

But Vinny went on: "Look at yourself. I'm being true to you right now. It pains me, man, what you're becoming, you coming in hot about hating your life. Before Ming Peou died, I didn't hear from you for weeks, haven't seen you for months, and you're asking me what I've been doing? Look, I've been doing the thing, what we've always agreed we were going to do. I moved to Oakland just to live it! And, like, I'm just making sure we aren't wasting time, you know? With fucking nonsense. Please, when we get Ming Peou's money—me, you, Molly—you won't need this Stanford bullshit."

"Stop bringing up this fucking money! Why don't you look at yourself? What the fuck are you doing? We were kids when we made that pact, and now you're a goddamn poster child for cultural appropriation. Acting like you're some badass Cambo gangster. Like it's still the nineties and shit? Like, your skin's brown, I'll give you that, but you're not Black. Not at all. So, stop fooling yourself."

Darren regretted the words as soon as he'd spoken them. Sometimes he just couldn't stop himself from being hurtful. It came with loving comedy. Anything could feed a punch line. Everything was fair game.

"Damn," Vinny said. "I don't know what to do with that, what you just—"

"Well, I'd leave you alone, but we need to get home for the funeral." Darren crossed his arms onto the bar, rested his head against his own clammy limbs. How did they end up here? Had this always been their dynamic? Darren didn't think so, but despite tons of memories he shared with his cousin, neither could he say, with certainty, that it wasn't.

"Man, stop playing," Vinny said to the counter. Then: "Should we have another drink?"

And Darren thought, *Now's the time*. If he were to ask Vinny about "Sachkrok Thom," to try to clarify the relationship between those lyrics and the truth, here was his opportunity. Only, it didn't feel right. The timing was off. His comedy chops might've been rusty, but he could always sense the right moment for a punch line, an aside, an interjection or tangent. Beyond being cousins, beyond growing up in the same town—because there were plenty of other cousins around, after all, other Cambo prohs whose parents had also survived genocide—this was what bonded Darren and Vinny together. Both cousins had always felt attuned to the rhythm of their shared experience. Whether telling jokes or making music, they knew well the importance of timing.

"Let's just go back to your place," Darren said.

"Okay," Vinny said, "but first—I have a proposition."

Darren lifted his head. "Yeah?"

"I want you to come on tour with me," Vinny said, his energy now forcing his cousin to make eye contact with him, his tone serious, more serious than anyone—not Darren, not Molly, not the other Khmai Kong Rappers—ever expected him to be. "This fall, aight? I'll be all over the country, hitting up venues left and right. We're gonna release a full album, with a real record label, and I want you there for it."

"That's amazing," Darren said, the lights in the room swirling around him in a drunken dance. "It really is. But, like—what would I do on this tour? Be your groupie? Wash your feet like you're that giant Buddha statue on the top of that mountain?"

"Man, just think about it for a second," Vinny said, "how baller it would be. This is what we've been working for our whole lives. My life's about to skyrocket, and I want you there with me. Us cousins, taking over the world. You opening shows with jokes, warming up the crowds, then me finishing them off with some rhymes. We'd kill it together and, like . . . I need you."

"I—fuck—I can't just quit my life. Not this second."

"Oh." Then, something under his breath. Then, rubbing the sides of his head, as though parsing a computational error. "Guess we can just . . . go, then."

"I'll think about it, though, I swear."

"Don't sweat it." Vinny pushed his stool back. "You know I'm not about deadlines or shit. Just let me know before I win Best New Artist at the Grammys." He stood up and slapped Darren on the back in that way of his. Rough, but with a touch of intimacy. That was how Vinny approached life. He could rage against the world with the best of them, but he was still a softie in the end, a heart-on-his-sleeves kind of guy, an all-my-tattoos-have-heartwarming-backstories kind of rapper. And Darren, almost the inverse of that—a recovering emo preteen who used to write poetry about his crushes and, even today, was sometimes oversensitive, but always with a blunt, sarcastic tone, a caustic nihilism seething under his words, a punch line waiting for the kill.

The cousins knew these things about each other, had felt confident in that knowledge. But as they walked out of the club, they became aware of a shift in each other's temperament. They were growing older; that was obvious. What hadn't been, at least until tonight, was how this maturing, this adjusting of what they loved in one another, entailed a reconciliation, a complete grappling, with what they had become and were becoming.

—

THE NEXT MORNING, THE SUN floating just above the Oakland Hills, Vinny woke up still high off the crowd's enthusiasm from the previous night. Rapping song after song, he had expelled everything hoarding up space in his lungs. He loved inhabiting the silence that hovered in the air after a performance. Loved this silence almost as much as the music itself. He felt as though each silence were different. You could master the song so well, it always sounded the same, but the silence afterward would still come out however it wanted, like it had to do with something more mysterious than your own voice. And if his favorite silence was the one following a music set, the empty space of a venue after an audience had cleared, then the quiet of an early morning, a day not yet started, was surely a close second. From his floorboard queen mattress, he examined the ceiling, took in the expanse of white stucco bumps. Then he got up, left his sparse bedroom, and walked out into the living room.

Vinny felt happy to see Darren still asleep on the couch. He wanted his cousin always to be passed out on his couch after a night of drinking. Standing over Darren, Vinny stared down into his cousin's face. He looked so unhappy, even sleeping, his forehead creased with lines. Or were those actually wrinkles, the first signs of aging? Was there a difference between getting old and looking unhappy? That is, if you already were unhappy, would the age show up as anything different? Or was it that the older you got, the harder it was to keep unhappiness off your face?

"Jesus Christ," Darren yelled, waking up to find Vinny, appearing as a shadow covered in tattoos, right above him.

"We gotta go," Vinny said, brushing off any hurt he might have felt at not being immediately recognized.

An hour later, they were on the 580, with Vinny driving his same 1990 Corolla, Darren in the passenger seat, Kelvin and Rithy sleeping in the back. When they finally merged onto the I-5, Vinny opened the center console and pulled out a joint. He handed it to Darren. "There's a lighter in there, too."

"Should we be smoking right now?"

"It's just a straight shot on the highway."

"Yeah, but—aren't we seeing the family, like, for the first time since Ming Peou died?"

"Exactly. We're gonna need to be high."

A NOTE ON THE HISTORY OF CAMBOTOWN FUNERALS

FICTION, FROM *STRAIGHT THRU CAMBOTOWN*

Darren and Vinny were cruising back home, and now, before our Cambo prohs merge onto the 405 and then the 710, where their shadows will be flitting across the very lane where Peou died, it's worth digressing to pay homage to what awaits them in Cambotown. Given their impending and official mourning, even I have to ask myself: What stream of history were the cousins about to step into, for the first time, as unknowing adults? What invisible current will be knocking them into the rapids of life, and toward what exactly will they be rushing forward?

The first Mas and Gongs to face death in the United States were primarily concerned with accruing enough old-school karma to ensure that nothing as horrible as an autogenocide would strike them in the new reincarnated lives they had ahead of them. In terms of authentic Buddhist traditions, they demanded their funerals be equipped with the works—a whole week of every close relative sleeping together on the floor of the deceased's home, burning as much incense as possible, an army of monks (even the monks known to be assholes, the ones who greeted templegoers by blowing cigarette smoke into their faces), fulfillment of the divine requirement for grandsons to shave their heads and live in the temple with the monks for at least three days, subsisting on nothing but cold rice and the smell of ash and enough home-cooked food to feed the entirety of Cambotown to nourish both its bodies and ghosts, its past and future souls, its every generation for all the decades to come.

As the years went by, though, it became harder to accommodate these traditions. Some Cambos had second and third jobs to work. Others had become too accustomed to their luxuries of air-conditioning and extra-soft mattresses and premium cable. Sleeping on the ground with thirty other relatives for a weeklong wake was hardly sustainable, especially when so many Cambos were plagued with PTSD-fueled nightmares—or even just sleep apnea—disorders that caused them to scream in the middle of the night, to gasp for air amid their dreams. And as generations of new Cambo-Americans enlarged each family, funeral homes stopped being so lenient. It was one thing, in the 1980s, when a party of thirty Cambos rolled into a funeral home, took off their shoes, and started droning unintelligible chants that rang through the entire neighborhood, but when thirty mourning Cambos increased to fifty, and then one hundred, and then several hundred, it became a different story.

With these difficulties came a lingering doubt that these traditions were worth keeping, a skepticism of whether anyone could actually remember with any accuracy what was and wasn't in line with true Khmer, true Buddhist, true Cambo-gangsta values, and a disbelief in the entire premise of reincarnation or karma in the face of Americanized teenagers who were taking AP Chemistry and Biology, who learned about scientific concepts, such as evolution and the laws of thermodynamics, on their way to becoming rational, educated members of U.S. society. By the time of Peou's death, the point of praying for a week straight for the dead, among other funeral rites, had slipped from our grasp, remaining out of reach while still taunting us with its presence, like a fish tangled in a line, thrashing to evade the fisherman's hands, trying to jump back into the ever-elusive depths of the ocean beyond.

But with this skepticism came a contingent of Ohms, Mings, and Pous determined to combat this loss of culture, to overcome what they saw as an endemic amnesia. This led to impressive feats of overcompensation. The inability to find willing funeral homes to accommodate their needs prompted the tripling of the amount of authentic Khmer food prepared as offerings for the spirits of the afterlife, those poor suckers stuck between death and reincarnation. Plates of prahok were left to rot even further at the base of altars, the stench of fermented fish mixing with the aroma of incense. Parents began forcing grandsons of the deceased to stay in the temple not for the traditional week, but often for almost a month. Once, a friend of mine refused this obligation as a grandson, explaining that he was an atheist and also that he was not about to shave his head just weeks before prom. In response, his mom brought a monk home to live in my friend's room, evicting him from his own bed for what turned out to be years, as two weeks into this arrangement, the monk decided to forgo his Buddhist calling. "My name is now Bradley," the monk stated, and naturally, my friend's mom felt too bad for Bradley to turn him out into the streets.

The next phase in the trajectory of Cambo funerals was open competition. Middle-aged Cambos started throwing funerals the way one would a wedding, say, or a graduation party—lavishly enough to prove they were better, richer, and more enlightened than the rest; not only were they the most Cambodian, but they also had the money to actualize this Cambo-ness. One year, a family hired a live band to accompany the Buddhist chants intoned during prayers. Another family flew famous monks straight from the homeland to grace Cambotown with the authority of their presence, the authenticity of their blessings. At the funeral of my second cousin's Gong, the eldest son of the deceased supposedly paid thousands of dollars to import supposed holy water from the secret wells of Angkor Wat. That same eldest son ended his eulogy for his beloved mother by forcing this holy water down his own throat, which sent him straight to the bathroom, where he stayed for the remainder of the funeral, shitting his brains out.

Planning a Cambo funeral, this is all to say, meant plunging into a deep chasm of conflicting cultures and shifting value systems, forced assimilation to standard American practices, superstitious paranoia about karmic destinies tempered by a burgeoning nihilism toward a universe that allowed millions of Cambo deaths, and competitive one-upmanship to prove the prominence and economic legitimacy of one's family unit. Imagine, then, the anticipation, the buildup, the utter trepidation thundering through Cambotown when it came to planning Peou's funeral. She had been the underlying adhesive keeping Cambotown together, after all, the very lynchpin of the Circle of Money.

It would have to be the funeral of all funerals, the party of the year, and in planning this event, Peou's older sisters drove themselves, each other, everyone around them absolutely insane. Not only did Ming Won and Ming Nary have to worry about traditions, honoring Peou's deep legacy, preparing food for hundreds of guests, and trying to determine whether they trusted Darren and Vinny to stay in the temple without embarrassing them, even as they coped with their own grief and pulled together the thousands of dollars to cover the funeral costs, but they were also well aware of the fact that every Ming and Ma in Cambotown was now hovering over them, waiting to sink their teeth into each minor mistake, before shaking their heads and whispering, *What a shame. Peou deserved better than what those two sisters call a funeral.*

MOLLY (AND PEOU)

FICTION, FROM *STRAIGHT THRU CAMBOTOWN*

The morning before the funeral, Molly woke up to an explosion of clanging metal; sharp, aggressive chopping; and women screaming. Immediately, she pulled the sheets over her head, massaged her temples, kept tracing those tiny circles. At twenty-five, Molly still hated mornings with the same intensity she had as a teenager. She had resigned herself long ago to never being a morning person, had always woken up feeling the ridiculous shame of existing, the shame of taking up space in this corrupt world, the shame of not being grateful that she was indeed alive, that she had been conceived by her parents in spite of higher powers hell-bent on punishing some kinds of people and not others. And it didn't help that this morning, louder than all that was crowding her mind, she heard her mother yelling, "Stupidhead! Stupidhead! Stupidhead!"

Finally, she worked up the nerve to throw herself from the

safety of her twin bed. Then she marched down the hallway to meet the day head-on.

In her mother's tiny kitchen, Molly found a dozen middle-aged women crowded between the two counters. Cracking open coconuts in the corner, with only a dollar-fifty meat cleaver, was Ohm Yey, Molly's old babysitter, who used to pin her down whenever Molly felt sick, coining her child-sized back with Tiger Balm until the throbbing pain of this intervention overpowered the discomfort of her mild symptoms. Not far from her, Ming Vee (the woman who called Ming Won several times a day to complain about her mother-in-law) and Ohm Lee (the devout Buddhist rumored to be having an affair with a monk) stood in front of a giant pot on the stove, throwing spices and kreun into their salaw machu, the whiff of lemongrass and garlic slapping Molly fully awake. Scattered throughout, meanwhile, chopping vegetables and rolling egg rolls and skewering beef into sach ko jakak, were women Molly had known all her life without ever committing their names to memory. She knew them as "Sam's depressed mom," "the Phnom Penh Noodle lady," "The lady who wears too much fake Gucci," and so on. And finally, at the center of the kitchen, were Ming Won and Ming Nary, each waving wooden ladles.

"STUPIDHEAD!" Ming Won shouted for what must have been the twentieth time that morning. "I don't care what you think about anything."

"You think I don't know my own baby sister!" Ming Nary cried. "Peou's favorite dessert was bai denap, not babaw poat!"

"Favorite dessert?! Are you an IDIOT? I have two hundred people to feed for the bun. We don't have time to soak sticky rice. We don't even have mangos or durian!"

"She just died! I want to eat my baby sister's favorite dessert." Just then, Ming Nary dropped her ladle and brought her hands to her face. She looked as though she were about to collapse, so Molly rushed to her aunt's side.

"Mai," Molly said, wrapping Ming Nary's arm around her shoulder, "can you stop screaming at everyone?!"

"Oun! What are you doing here?!" Ming Won yelled, pointing her wooden ladle at her daughter. "Did you write the speech yet? I know you didn't. You're so lazy. Ever since you moved back home, all you do is sleep. Stop wasting time and go write."

Ming Nary patted Molly on the back. "Molly, don't waste time," she said. "Make sure you write a good eulogy, too. We're counting on you."

"Oh my god," Molly said. "How did this become an attack on me?"

"Go!" Ming Won said. "Go write! Leave! You're in the way!"

"I already wrote it!" Molly yelled as she stormed out of the kitchen.

Back in her bedroom, Molly sat at her desk and pressed her fingers into her temples, tracing more circles. She took deep breaths and told herself that everyone processes death in their own way, and even her psycho mother had a right to express her grief in whatever fucked-up way she needed.

She stared at the eulogy-writing guide she had printed from an online website after googling "writer's block eulogy original heartfelt." There was a series of brainstorming questions that Molly had started to answer before giving up.

What are qualities you would ascribe to the deceased?

"Inspiring, hardworking, cutthroat, absurd."

What's a funny anecdote you remember about the deceased?

"She wasn't a funny person, but that was why she was so funny."

How has the deceased impacted your life?

"How hasn't she?"

And so on.

Earlier that week, Molly had actually finished writing a eulogy, but she hated it. She hated it while she wrote it, she hated it after finishing it, and this hate only festered as the funeral approached. It felt empty and vapid, what she had written, as if she knew nothing about Peou, as if she hadn't grown up wanting to be exactly like her Ming.

Molly placed her forehead on the desk. "What do you want me to say?" she whispered into the cold wood. "How do you want to be remembered?"

—

EVEN BEFORE WRITING THIS EULOGY, Molly had been in a rut. Ever since moving back home, two months before Peou's death, she had been feeling like her old college roommate, the rich one who slumped into sophomore year without the ability to produce serotonin, her summer "interning in the fashion industry" having been code for taking too much MDMA while crashing parties in New York City. (Once, when Molly was complaining that her roommate never left the apartment, that all this roommate did was rattle on and on about her undiagnosed anxiety, Darren joked that Molly's roommate had traded dependence on one Molly for another.) Now, stuck in Cambotown, after five glorious years in NYC and two years that totally kicked her ass, Molly felt completely undone, existential, and, like her old roommate, panicked that her old passions just didn't hit the same as before.

She had a bachelor's degree in "Illustrating the Political Self" from the Gallatin School of Individualized Study at NYU, but she hadn't drawn anything in months, not even her "political self." She had recently been "let go" from her nonprofit gig and replaced by two unpaid social media interns, which prompted her now ex-boyfriend to accuse her of "lacking direction," not caring about "their future," and "stifling" him. She was twenty-five and owed $200K in student loans, with an extra $5K in credit card debt from an ill-advised semester studying painting abroad in Florence. Molly was not doing well. Plus, all her stuff—books, art, wardrobe—had yet to arrive in Cambotown from New York City. She'd tried to save money by mailing boxes through the regular post office, instead of hiring a moving company, and now everything was, according to several federal workers on the phone, nowhere to be found. The symbolism was not lost on her.

On top of this, the only saving grace of being in Cambotown had died.

Oh, Peou—the beacon of hope for Molly, the only woman in Cambotown happily unmarried, without kids, not just content to devote her life to her ambitions but proud of it. The week before Peou died, Molly had approached her about a job, as she needed to start paying back her student loans. How much longer could she lounge around the house, depressed, unmotivated to even put on real pants, getting yelled at by Ming Won?

Her Ming Peou, of course, came through. Or, she would have, had Molly not been so stubborn. When Molly told Peou about her need to find a job, Peou laughed through the phone. "You're better than being a cashier at Happy Donuts," she said, before offering Molly the keys to her empire. "Come work for me. I'll teach you."

"Except, I really just want something temporary, Ming. I don't wanna be stuck here forever."

"And what's wrong with that?"

"You sound just like my mom."

"Maybe you should listen to her. If two people are saying the same thing—"

"I'm tired of explaining myself. I'm an adult, and the world's just . . . different, okay? I can't just live the way you guys do. It's unsustainable. And it doesn't make any sense. I mean, Ming, your job is literally illegal."

Silence.

Then: "Ming, I need to go."

This last conversation, looping in her head, blocked Molly from drafting a better eulogy.

—

AT NOON, MOLLY WAS STILL at her desk, still failing to rewrite her eulogy, when the only surviving constants of her life, her Cambo prohs, burst into the room.

Molly jumped from her chair. "Don't fucking scare me like that!"

"Baby sis," Vinny said. "Mai told us to make sure you're working. So, are you working?"

"Ugh, I can't with her!"

"Tell us something new," Darren said, and Molly let out a bitter laugh.

"Well, if you aren't working," Vinny said, "you gotta come with us. We've been assigned a mission from the control center. Mai's directing an orchestra out there. She's preparing for war. She's—"

"Fool, stop with the mixed metaphors, all right?" Darren interjected. "We're picking up nom lort from the Lort Guy, that's all."

"Man, I'm pumped. Fuck—I love those green worms. Shit is some heavenly tapioca coconut abyss."

"Fuck, you both are high," Molly said, before looking back at the papers on her desk, the open journal filled with self-portraits over a year old, the unused drawing pens scattered over the cheap wooden surface.

Ming, I just don't know what to write. I need help. I don't know what to do.

Come work for me. I'll teach you.

"And that's a problem?" Darren said.

"The real question, baby sis," Vinny said. "Do you *also* wanna get high?"

Molly crossed her arms and looked Darren and Vinny over. They hadn't changed at all. The way Vinny stuck out his neck and bobbed his head while talking, like every sound from his mouth was a dance anthem. How Darren never focused on one person, never looked anyone in the eye, was always scanning the room for external validation, an audience. The three of them standing in her childhood room, Molly felt transported to their high school years, except they were muted versions of themselves, without her dyed hair and combat boots, their oversized T-shirts and baggy jeans. It was hard for Molly to imagine that both Vinny and Darren, as unchanged as they were, had actually found success in their careers, their passions. Unlike her.

"I have to put on real pants," she said, expelling them from her room.

Later, in the backseat of the Corolla she'd always hated for its lack of air-conditioning, Molly found herself crammed between a pair of doofuses she had known all her life and never once taken seriously. "You two have nothing better to do than, like, follow my brother around?"

"*Man*, Vinny," said Kelvin, the one who spoke with a lisp and seemed more pathetic with every pound of muscle he gained. "Why's your sister such a bitch?"

"Don't call her a bitch, fool," said Rithy, the one who was too nice to Molly, making her feel both infantilized and objectified. "You're not even supposed to say 'bitch' anymore. Right, Molly?"

"I don't care what you call me."

"What she said," Vinny replied.

Molly looked down at the notebook on her lap. She tried thinking of something heartfelt and profound to write about Peou, but couldn't think of anything. Then the pain struck her.

"Fuck, does anyone have Advil?"

"Who just carries Advil around?" Darren asked.

If not for the incipient migraine, Molly would have rolled her eyes. Her older cousin and brother were still overgrown boys, and Molly felt, briefly, a flare of that same bitterness toward Darren's and Vinny's relative successes, but she brushed the feeling away, as she always did. She really did want the best for them. "Well, can we stop by a Rite Aid, then?"

One hand on the steering wheel, Vinny started rummaging through the center console, then pulled out a half-smoked joint and a lighter and handed them to Molly. "Here," he said, "all the medicine you need."

Molly stared at the joint. She was hardly a fan of marijuana, having spent the better part of her teenage years annoyed that Darren and Vinny were always high, but for the past two months, and this week especially, she had been teetering on such a precarious tightrope of stable emotions that . . . who knew? Maybe it would help. The piercing pain grew sharper between her eyes as it spread over her entire face.

"This isn't gonna be enough," Molly said, before lighting the joint and inhaling some smoke. *I'm sorry*, she then thought, as she placed her notebook in the webbed pocket behind the passenger seat. *I know this looks bad.*

Come work for me. I'll teach you.

I'm sorry, Ming. I'm sorry. I'm sorry.

"Anyway, I'm dropping these dopes off," Vinny said, "so let's just ask Kelvin's mom to give us some of those Big Pharma drugs you're fiending for. Kelvin's house is stocked like a bunker for Y2K. Can't ask Rithy's mom, 'cause she's, like, off the chain. Badass lady, but damn, she's got zero shits together. Yo, Rithy, remember that time your mom kicked your dad out of the house because she caught him playing that online casino game? Like, how hilarious was that? She didn't realize it was just a gambling game, with, like, virtual fake money, not real gambling with real money."

"Fool, course I remember," Rithy said. "It's my life."

"Fake money or not," Darren said, "Cambos are just crazy like that. Everyone's a walking case study for PTSD. We're all desperate to protect ourselves from anything that could be considered bad. At a certain point, we aren't even making sense anymore. Ever notice how we burn fake money for our ancestors, yet we believe in reincarnation? Like, what the fuck's that shit? The afterlife is this current life we are living, right? And here we are acting all Chinese and shit, burning fake money for the spirits. I mean, how does no one realize the paradox in this? How does no one ever step back and wonder if the afterlife is just literally life, like, if reincarnation means we're reborn into new bodies, then where the hell's this magical ash money our descendants burned for us? Shit makes no sense. Sooner or later, we're gonna start attending Christian people church and the temple, just in case heaven and hell do exist. Fuck, why not just add being Jewish in there. Sprinkle in some Islam. We gotta prepare for the end of society and adopt every fucking belief system possible."

"Man," Kelvin said to the car, "this is why I love this guy." He wrapped his arm around Darren's chest from behind the passenger seat. "Fool just, like, goes off. Sayin' crazy shit about being Cambodian and the world. He's a trip."

"Fool, get off me," Darren said, elbowing Kelvin's arm away.

"I know Ming Peou just died," Vinny said, "but you're getting existential as fuck."

"I've been reading too much Kant."

"The fuck you saying?"

"I don't care where we go," Molly said. "Just get me some Advil."

"Then leggggoooooooooo," Vinny said, putting on his fake Gucci sunglasses, exhaling a giddy desperate laugh. "I want some green worms in my tummy."

He made a sharp right onto Gardenia Street, everyone shifting in their seats, and for a brief moment, Molly thought this could jolt their world back to normal, dislodge it from the grasp of their communal grief, that when the car realigned and they were sitting upright again, Peou would no longer be dead. They would all be happy, could live in that illusion of unfulfilled promise, where their favorite Ming would always be there to bail them out.

Come work for me. I'll teach you.

"Fucking shit, Vinny," Darren said, clutching the car's roof handle, and Molly knew nothing had changed.

—

TWO MONTHS LIVING IN CAMBOTOWN again, yet this was the first time in years Molly had been on Gardenia Street. The cramped single-story houses flashed through her line of vision, with their porches and chipped pastel paint, the patches of dead, yellow grass out front. A few of them had Foreclosure Sale signs posted, the block letters aggressive and blunt. They used to live here, before Ming Won and Ming Nary got jobs at the DMV. After Darren's father, Pou Song, returned to Cambodia (bailing on the Cambo project of American resettlement once he saved enough money for a second family, a new start in a destroyed place where the land was cheap as long as there were no leftover bombs to demine), Ming Nary and Darren lived in their house, where Ming Peou had also lived. For five years, they all lived together, and it was the happiest time of Molly's childhood, having three mothers and two older brothers for the price of one. The constant presence of Darren, Ming Nary, and Ming Peou was enough to make up for her own ignorant, shitty father.

Maybe it was the growing migraine, or the impending doom of Peou's funeral, that final goodbye that felt pointless and false, but as Molly walked across the unkempt lawn of Kelvin's mother's house, her attention fixed upon a black Lexus SUV parked a few spaces behind Vinny's Corolla and then upon the man sitting in the driver's seat wearing a Dodgers cap—probably Chinese Cambodian—though she couldn't place him. Paranoia trickled into the pain of her migraine. Why did this man stick out to her? What was his relevance to her world?

Then she was on the ground, crying. It was the first time she had cried since the day of Peou's death. Trying desperately to recall some long-lost detail, she felt the gaps of her own memory, the lingering shadows of the past that had stretched into her family's present, into Cambotown, these shadows she recognized but didn't quite understand, even as they were beginning to fade, to diminish, along with her memory of Peou herself.

How fucked-up! How unfair! To feel her Ming dying, yet again, in her mind, just days after that original, earth-shattering heartbreak. To grieve a loved one is to suffer and witness an infinite cycle of recursive deaths, Peou's kmouys would learn, again and again.

Darren was the first to come to Molly's side. He lifted her into an upright, sitting position, then sat down next to her, propping her up with his body like they were kids again, forced to pray with the monks during Cambodian New Year, enduring the leg cramps only by leaning against one another's side. "It's okay," he said. "Everything's all right."

"Shit, lemme get that Advil," Vinny said, before running into the house with Kelvin and Rithy.

Molly sat there, tears streaming down her face. Chest heaving, she could barely breathe. She felt engulfed by her surroundings. All her life, Molly had felt a sense of direction, destined, she thought, to exhibit her self-portraits all over the globe, in New York City, London, Tokyo, and Paris (where she had planned to handcuff herself to some immovable object at the Louvre, as a political demonstration meant to shed light on France's colonization of Cambodia, how Cambo girls like her deserved a place in the most esteemed permanent collection in the world). She had always thought her life would be epic, that she would be known for her art, her speeches at protests, her general badassery. And now, here she was: crying on the street where she'd been conceived.

"I guess we can just sit here . . . outside . . . on the ground," Darren said, in that stilted tone he used when trying to be funny. "After a while, I think, if we stay here long enough, we get squatters' rights." Darren raised his eyebrows and smiled, and the pressure behind Molly's eyes eased somewhat.

"Fuck, I'm high," Molly said.

"No shit."

Molly studied her cousin's face. His bushy eyebrows lacking any curvature, flat as his self-deprecating voice. His eyes turned downward slightly—like a puppy dog's, Ming Nary used to say—which steeped his expressions with a weariness beyond his young age. Then she glanced behind her, before turning back to Darren. She gestured for him to lean closer to her face.

"Hey," she whispered, "you recognize that black Lexus there?"

Darren raised his head, looked straight at the car. "Am I supposed to just remember cars now?" he said loudly, obnoxiously.

Molly grabbed him by the shirt and pulled him down. "Fuck, Darren, be discreet."

"Yeah, well, it's pretty tacky to be driving a car that nice on this street."

"That's not the point. Doesn't it seem weird that there's a guy just . . . sitting there? Like, he's just there. Doesn't he have anywhere else to be?"

Just then, Vinny loped out of the house, his two henchmen trailing after him. "Kelvin's mom came through with the drugs," Vinny said, plopping himself right onto the ground. "She also hooked you up with some 7UP because, according to her scientific research as a paranoid Cambo mom, lemon-lime carbonation synthesizes Advil to, like, maximal potential."

Molly popped the Advil into her mouth, threw her head back as she poured 7UP down her throat. Then, just as she was about to ask Vinny the same questions concerning the car, the man in the Dodgers hat pulled out from the curb and drove away.

"Fuck," Molly said.

"You scared the Lexus away," Darren said.

"What's going on?" Vinny asked.

"Molly thinks we're being followed."

"Yo, that's pretty funny."

"Guys, I'm being serious," Molly said. "It's was just, like, fucking weird."

"It's the weed, baby sis. Like, this is some extra-strength, medical-grade shit."

"Yeah," Rithy said. "I smoked too much of this shit the other week and lost my mind. Legit thought I was gonna fall into my phone screen and, like, into some new dimension."

"Team," Vinny said, springing to his feet, "we need to stop getting distracted from the mission! Okay? Plus, we got new orders, and fuck us if we fuck up Ming Peou's funeral. We need that lort!"

"Yeah, my mom," Kelvin chimed in, "she found out you guys are hitting the Lort Guy up, and now she wants us to get a palm tree pod from his backyard."

"Why the fuck does she need a palm seed?" Molly asked.

"Woman, I don't know," Kelvin said. "Probably for the funeral."

"Palm seeds are for weddings," Molly said. "Fucking idiot."

"I dunno, someone's always getting married," Darren

said, standing up and then helping Molly to her feet. "For every funeral there's, like, five weddings, you know?"

"It's motherfucking wedding season!" Vinny yelled, sprinting back to his car.

They piled back into Vinny's Corolla and drove three blocks, parking on Lemon Avenue, where they all stared at the faded pink house owned by the Lort Guy's mother. The blinds locked upward in every window, the driveway empty, the house scowled a poker face, projected an eerie silence, at least when compared to the other residences on the block, which had driveways overfilled with tandem-parked cars.

"No one's home?" Rithy said.

"Well, someone's gotta be there," Darren said. "Like ten whole persons live in this house, I'm pretty sure."

After ringing the doorbell to no response, the five of them were about to call it a day, resign themselves to returning to their mothers empty-handed, proving once again their utter ineptitude and immaturity, when Molly noticed a flutter in the window blinds adjacent to the front door and a wary eye peeking outside to scope them out.

Molly banged on the door. "Hello! Is someone there?"

The door cracked open, and a sliver of a sixty-year-old woman's face appeared—the Lort Guy's mother. Then a rush of words: "What do you want?"

"We're here to pick up the nom lort," Molly said. "The nom lort for Ming Peou's funeral."

The Lort Guy's mother's bloodshot eyes widened, and her head jolted backward. "NO ONE IS HERE," she said, slamming the door shut.

Their jaws dropped, confusion stifling their words.

"What the fuck was that?" Darren said.

Another moment passed, and they still hadn't moved from the porch. Then the Lort Guy's mother materialized in the window through the blinds.

"NO ONE IS HERE," she yelled again, more or less audibly.

"OKAY. WE GOT IT," Vinny responded with mock exasperation.

Back in Vinny's car, the five of them, still shaken from that previous antagonism, were at a loss for what to do next, where they would go from there, how they would keep distracting themselves from all there was to ruminate over and sink into forever. Kelvin and Rithy scrolled through the messages on their phones. Vinny kept tapping the steering wheel, punctuating the mood with an anxious beat. Darren's legs quivered, like they had been doing in his philosophy seminars, and when they started to bump up against the dashboard, the sound messing with Vinny's tapping beat, Vinny slapped Darren's left thigh, held it in place, before saying, "Can you fucking stop that?"

Darren smacked Vinny's hand away, firing a hostile expression to go with the gesture, but didn't say anything, so the two cousins just stared each other down, Darren with his touch-me-again-at-your-own-risk-I-dare-you front and Vinny reciprocating a bemused look of yeah-sure-let's-fight-I-got-nothing-to-do-right-now-but-fuck-up-my-dear-cousin.

"Jesus," Molly said, "what gives?" She had been wading through her confusion about the Lort Guy's mother, leaning forward in her middle seat, her hands fishing through the roots of her hair, on either side of her head, with arms circling counterclockwise, periodically, rhythmically, a fruitless resetting, before she was dragged back to reality by Darren and Vinny. Sure, of course, she had been thinking, Peou's job as the Counter meant that some Cambos found her presence uneasy. Especially if those Cambos had owed a significant sum of money. But wasn't Peou the very person trusted to make sure everyone got paid? That no one was cheated by anyone too selfish to pay back their dues. Hadn't Peou had everyone's best interests in mind? That's how the Circle of Money was supposed to work, right? What the hell was up with the Lort Guy's mother, who, as far as Molly knew, had been decently close to Peou, to her family?

"Ah, fuck," Kelvin abruptly said. "I can't go home without a palm pod. My mom'll kill me."

Vinny slapped both his thighs in excitement and turned around to face Kelvin, Molly, and Rithy. "Naw, we fucking got this!"

After parking farther down the street so that his car was no longer in the line of sight of the Lort Guy's mother, Vinny led their pack to the side of the faded pink house, all of them scaling the walls and ducking underneath windows. Molly and Darren were skeptical of Vinny, as always. But it was too hot to stay in the car. Besides, who were they to question Vinny's motives, his manic energy, which they faintly recognized as a coping mechanism not only for Peou's death, but also for being back in Cambotown, where everyone had always underestimated him next to Darren and even Molly. They stopped at the locked fence gate leading to the backyard, still crouching, as perpendicular to the fence was another window. Looking up from the ground, they saw palm fronds striping the sky. Streaks of green cut through the clouds.

"Baby sis," Vinny said, "we're gonna throw you over this fence, all right?"

"What the fuck? It's your plan; *you* climb the fucking tree."

"You're the girl here. Better for you to be harvesting those pods."

"Yeah, versus, like, a thug covered in tattoos," Darren said with a monotone barely concealing his annoyance toward Vinny, this situation, the whole ordeal. "Plus, you're the best at climbing."

"That was ten years ago," Molly said. "We aren't kids anymore."

"We're always kids in Cambotown," Vinny said, smirking, staring at Molly until she cracked.

"Fine—god—just keep watch."

"No one'll give a fuck if they see you climbing this tree, anyway," Kelvin said. "Not on this side of the fence."

"Yeah, it's the Lort Guy's mom you gotta worry about," Rithy added. "So, keep watch yourself."

Molly felt her migraine pound against her face. This is what I get, she thought, for hanging with these fools. Then, remembering all the times she accompanied Peou on her collections, she wondered: *How did Ming Peou spend her whole life dealing with dumb Cambo men? How did she manage to trust them to own up to their debts?*

"C'mon, c'mon," Vinny said. "Rithy, throw her over already."

Stepping into Rithy's palms, Molly was launched high enough to grab the top of the fence. Then she vaulted over with only some initial struggle, but, when landing, she buckled under her own inertia, slamming a knee into the concrete of the garden pathway. A shock pierced into her bone and spread through her right leg. With her hands, she muffled her gasp of pain.

Come work for me. I'll teach you how to do this right. Not like an idiot.

The pain in her knee waned, thank god, as she climbed the palm tree, wrapping her thighs around its trunk and carefully locating grooves to place her hands. Planted near the back-left corner of the house, the tree was far enough from the fence—several strides away—for Molly to feel uneasy. If she turned her head, she had an oblique view into the house, through the sliding glass doors, and she checked periodically to see if the Lort Guy's mother had caught her trespassing, though she knew there was nowhere to run or hide, really, so the best course of action, were she caught, would be to complete her task, climb down the tree, and face the consequences.

Still, the higher she climbed, the uneasier she became, this uneasiness sublimating directly into rage—rage at her brother for convincing her to retrieve these pods (and not even for their own mother) and then rage at herself for agreeing to this absurd mission; at her very skin for its vulnerability to splinters; her stupid fucking brain for being prone to migraines; her culture for having use for the guts of palm tree pods because tradition dictated that people throw white pka slas at brides and grooms, as if older Cambos needed to be hurling or projecting anymore nonsense at their Cambo youths; and also, of course, at the Lort Guy, for being fucking MIA; and the Lort Guy's mother for making, like, zero sense; and finally, at the notion that apparently she was the only person who could be trusted to do tasks no one else wanted to do, such as scaling a palm tree, for instance, or writing a goddamn eulogy. By the time she reached the top, fronds slicing at the exposed spots of her body, Molly's pale brown face had reddened into the emergence of a blistering sunburn.

Gripping the trunk tighter with her legs, she struggled to dislodge a pod from its base. *These things are fucking giant*, she thought, before imagining herself pelting pods down at the Lort Guy's mother's house, at her brother and his henchmen and their dumbass luck in being rappers, at her overbearing mother and dickhead father. She wanted everyone to scramble and panic in fear of her thunderous barrage. She started to tear up again.

You can't take everything seriously, oun. It'll kill you.

Finally, the pod was in her hands, severed from the tree. She looked at the ground. From this angle, she could no longer see Vinny or Darren ducked behind the fence, yet she felt the vague sense of being watched, by them, by every house in the neighborhood, by all of Cambotown. She looked west and saw the shores of the beach, the horizontal slab of ocean. She thought about the fact that she'd barely visited the beach as a child, the perimeter between Cambotown and the rest of Long Beach having seemed all but impassable. From above, the five blocks of Cambotown, of pastel-colored buildings, appeared all-encompassing yet compressed and squat. For maybe the first time she could remember, having passed from the unquestioning devotion of childhood straight into the eternal resentment of adolescence and then straight into early adulthood's chronic avoidance—all the visits postponed, the holidays cut short—Molly's feelings toward Cambotown lacked... precision. Of course, she had felt abysmal when she first moved back from New York. But that was before Peou's death. Now she had no idea, really, not even how she should feel.

Forcing herself back into the task at hand, she threw the pod so that it landed softly onto a bush near the side of the house, then checked if anyone in the house had caught her atop the palm tree. Through one of the glass doors into the house's kitchen, she recognized the Lort Guy standing in front of the fridge. You could tell it was him. The premature potbelly. The awkward duck stance of his stumpy legs. The bald spot stamped onto the back of his head.

Is this how I'd turn out, Molly wondered, *if Ming Peou weren't dead, if I'd taken her up on her offer, if I dedicated myself to this town? Would I be living at home, almost forty, looking like... this?* Then it dawned on her—the Lort Guy standing in his kitchen, shoveling food into his mouth, even as his mother was covering for him, both of them refusing to engage with Molly's family. The only explanation Molly could think of for this refusal, though she couldn't gauge the deeper reasons, was Peou's death. Everything was out of order now, wasn't it?

She felt the lightheadedness of being elevated into the clouds, the gravity urging her toward the earth. Chills spread through her nerves, a numbing shock, even after she'd climbed down, even after she found herself back in Vinny's car, lodged between Rithy and Kelvin, a palm tree pod laid across their three laps. She couldn't shake the feeling that some inexorable force was at work, beneath the faded, sun-drenched surface of Cambotown, some tectonic shift about to split the very ground beneath their feet. And yet, within these unsettling chills, this growing paranoia, Molly felt an odd comfort, as though high up in that palm tree, she had retrieved a parcel of validation. It was small, yes, and infinitesimal compared to her grief. But, for now, it was enough.

—

LATER THAT NIGHT, MOLLY WAS sitting at her desk again, staring at that blank page in her notebook. She chewed a lock of her black hair, tapped her pen against the desk, itched at the spot where the threadbare interior of her sweatpants scraped her thigh. An hour had passed since she had sat down to work on the eulogy, all the words, sentences, and language dammed up against the reservoir walls of her mind. The Lort Guy stuffing his face, in open contempt of the funeral—his image consumed her. Eventually, she found herself marking the blank page. Barely even caring anymore. What did it matter? Slowly, a face formed in those scratches of ink, the roughness of that shading, the jagged sloppiness of her lines, all those stylistic flourishes, those bad habits her college teachers had tried to train right out of her practice.

There it was, that familiar face: high cheekbones; eyebrows an attack of angles; hair cropped above her broad shoulders, pushed behind ears; and then that pointed chin. Her eyes, a glimmer of condescension in the stare, pupils lifted, buoyed by the white of the sclera, to the ceiling of her eyelids. That look had made Molly feel protected as a child.

It was as though her Ming were always scoping out the space, the air, right above her head, the height she'd one day reach.

By the time the portrait had fully emerged, Molly was in tears, but this time her crying was just that—a spilling forth. No hyperventilating. No crushing weight in her chest. No feeling of nothingness seizing her mind. And when she finished, the cloudy water draining from her vision, it finally hit her, that indirect lightning of purpose. She turned the page, resting Peou's face in the confines of her notebook, and began writing.

> "All the good men died," Ming Peou often told me.
> When my mother first asked me to write this eulogy, that's the first thought that came to me. She first told me this after everyone found out about my first boyfriend, who was, I hate to admit, a few years older than me, an upperclassman in high school, who picked up his sister, one of my best friends at the time, from our middle school every afternoon. He and I never did anything, I swear. We mostly emailed each other love letters, innocent stuff, really. He'd talk about the vacations he'd whisk me away on, how he wanted to marry me, that he believed in true everlasting love, but one day my mother found my email open on our family computer, and of course she knew exactly how much older my boyfriend was than me, being friends with his mother, so naturally, as you can imagine, all hell broke loose.
> Then, when Ming Peou heard about him, these emails, she slapped me across the face, right in the

same spot my mother had slapped me the day before, because how could I degrade myself like that? How could I let a boy, who was almost a man, have power over me like that? How could I be so stupid to trust someone who could hurt me? Who wanted nothing but to fulfill his own selfish desires? Didn't I know not to trust men? "Oh, oun," she said, when I shook my head, unable to speak because I was sobbing, my cheek burning from her slap.

"All the good men died," she said.

"What do you mean?" I said.

"Back in the genocide," she said. "They worked them as slaves in the fields, tortured them, imprisoned them in S-Twenty-one and poured water over their clothed faces until they begged the soldiers to kill them, put them out of their misery. The teachers, the painters, the entrepreneurs that slowly accrued their wealth and were good to their wives and children, the intellectuals who went abroad to study in Taipei, New York, and Paris and were lured back to Cambodia by Pol Pot with promises of élite positions in policy, only to be kidnapped upon their first steps back in the homeland; the fabric weavers whose fingertips could unlock the magnificent colors and patterns of our past; the musicians who sang odes of our golden age; the architects that learned from the best French designers even as they evoked the silhouettes of those wats that were later bombed; the sculptors that shaped the curves of our Apsaras and carved Buddha's face into our memories so that we could still hold on to our beliefs when our world was reset into terror—they were all killed, even the men with glasses, who were trained to see the world in two different ways, blindly and clear-eyed, as Pol Pot had anyone with the red marks of a frame on their nose murdered.

"Pol Pot wanted his men to adhere to only one way of life, he didn't want beauty or history or culture or intelligence or morality or religion. Just servants to his greatness, his kingdom. Sure, he was Communist, but he was sick in the head, and his communism was to make everyone equal with the same sickness, and the ones who didn't get sick, all the good men, they were massacred. Now we have only men obsessed with power. Which means," Ming Peou then said, "the boys here, the prohs trying to be your boyfriend, you can't trust them. They don't have decent role models anymore. They will do anything, tell you anything, to get what they want. They don't believe in true love! How could they? The singers of true love had died. The artists who captured real beauty were dead. These prohs know nothing, and no one is teaching them, so you, as a woman, oun, you need to be careful, stay on guard, stay in control of every situation you walk into the best you can."

At the time, I thought Ming Peou was being dramatic, but now I can't help but see the truth in what she said. She never hated our men or boys. No, she loved everyone in our community deeply. But she recognized that it was up to Cambodian women to lead our community, to whip our men into shape and rear our children. She wanted to lead us into a new era of wealth. And I don't think I am exaggerating when I say that she's made a difference in the lives of everyone in this room. She's responsible for any amount of success I ever achieve. She's the reason why I did well in school, why I graduated from college.

But I want to focus on what Ming Peou meant for my fellow Cambo girls. I don't want to spend this time just talking about men. Ming Peou—she loved to lecture her kmouys: me, Darren, and Vinny. "Don't you know about Nokor Thom and Banteay Srei?" she'd say whenever Darren or Vinny bullied me. We always knew exactly what she meant, she repeated the story so many times, but we loved hearing her rants.

"In the old-old days," the story started, "when they were still building the ancient temples, there was a competition. A dare. The men would build a temple city, and the women would build their own. So, the men went to building, and they built the greatest city Cambodia ever saw. They carved hundreds of faces of Lokesvara, so that walking anywhere, you felt Buddha watching your every move. Nokor Thom was great, it was big, it was impressive. But the women, they took their sweet time. What was the rush? No one put a time limit on their dare. The women had nothing to prove, so they focused on building not the greatest temple, but the most beautiful. They used pink sandstone only their hands could shape. They spent years carving flowers into their statues, made sure each surface became a work of art, that the temple carried our history on its skin. Banteay Srei ended up so beautiful, it was called the art gallery of Angkor. And guess what happened to the great, big, old temple city of Nokor Thom, versus the smaller Banteay Srei. It was bombed a hundred times over during the war! Great, giant city. What good did it do? To be great? In the end, its greatness only made it a better target to be destroyed."

Ming Peou mourned the good men who died, but she still recognized how these men could have learned from their women counterparts. I will never be more grateful for anything than Ming Peou's willingness to recite us stories like the legend of Banteay Srei. She wasn't afraid to be contradictory. She gave us wisdom our parents wouldn't. Wisdom that no Cambo men would ever want the younger generations, especially us girls, to have, so scared they are that we should become empowered. That we would have a voice. That we wouldn't be afraid to see and speak paradoxical truths. That we would grow up to be another Peou Ros, another strong woman calling the shots, another woman who didn't tolerate any nonsense from men, who refused to be talked down to. Peou Ros was a force of nature. All the good men died, so we needed women like Ming Peou. And now, I am heartbroken to say, we have also lost a good woman. One of the best. May you rest in peace. We will always remember you, because, as far as I'm concerned, your legacy will never die.

DUPLEX

NONFICTION, ORIGINALLY PUBLISHED
IN *THE NEW YORKER*

I.
ARTIST'S STATEMENT ON METHODS AND HOME DEPOT

My stunt as a college art student in the early 2010s, Silicon Valley: tan workman jacket cut from canvas and held together with safety pins; tattered jeans my grandmother was always patching up without my asking; and cheap, red, faded sweatshirt I'd got at a secondhand store, in San Francisco's Mission District. (Years later, my boyfriend would scold me for staining that durable Hanes cotton with burrito grease.)

Every week, I dozed through lectures on the greatest hits of art history. Madonnas washed in egg tempera. The sfumato and steroided gods of the Renaissance. Jackson

Pollock dripping expensive oil paints with reckless abandon. Then I observed my peers mix oils and solvents into self-portraits of freakish realism. After my last class of the week, depending on how stressed I was about deadlines or impending studio critiques, I often drove to the colossal strip mall, the barricade—formed by Ikea and Home Depot and all the fast-food outlets—that separated the rich families of the San Francisco Peninsula, the élite and sheltered undergraduates, the tech workers and VC dudes, from the Latino and immigrant neighborhoods of East Palo Alto. It had a socioeconomic range much like that of my own community, sixty miles away, in another of California's many valleys.

I didn't waste tubes of paint, but I plowed through Roman Pro-880 Ultra Clear Strippable Wallpaper Adhesive. On each trip to Home Depot, I reasoned that I'd need one or two ten-dollar quarts. My estimates were consistently and wildly off base. Somehow, in my adherence to a modest budget, I'd cemented myself as the ideal customer of wallpaper glue.

The trip itself was crucial to my process. As was a method of print—transfer collaging that required wintergreen oil, free paper and ink from the campus media lab, a burnisher I'd stolen (and still have in my possession) from the studio facilities, and compulsive etching, which I'd do until my palms blistered or my old blisters tore into fresh cuts. Or until my mess of facsimiles cohered.

So, let's say that each of my visual art works began with a stroll down the commercial-paint aisle. Let's also say that home-improvement supplies and equipment reminded me of my father, which made me just insecure enough in my practice (which in turn made my ego just grandiose enough) to maintain a productive groove. It follows, then, that Dad factored heavily into my aesthetic. When I first learned the method for print transfers, I reproduced images of Dad looking disgruntled and forlorn. After applying a thin layer of wintergreen oil onto the back side of a xeroxed picture—mostly I used copies of a 120-color-film photograph I'd taken and developed—I scratched Dad's grainy face onto oversized pieces of paper. Finally, I added cartoon speech bubbles of his quotes and sayings. My favorite: "Do well in school for a good job, because you can't handle a hard one. You fall out of too many chairs."

Then I developed my own systematic routine for print transferring. I'd claim a corner of a vacant studio for the night. At my side I'd have two brayer rollers, a quart of wallpaper glue, a long stretch of butcher paper, and a stack of pictures, half of them neon—tinted reproductions of Khmer Rouge genocide photographs I'd made using gum arabic printmaking and Adobe Photoshop, the other half xeroxed copies of family photos. First, I dipped a brayer in glue and rolled it over the back side of a picture. Second, using a clean brayer, I rolled the picture onto the butcher paper. Repeating these steps, I assembled a cascade of overlapping and vivid tones, an expanse of personal archives interwoven with the killing fields. Then I hung the scrolls in the lobby of the art building, at parties in cooperative undergraduate housing, and on the walls of my dorm room, so that I could stare into my own vision when stoned.

Working with the wallpaper glue, I often thought of Dad's duplexes, the post-refugee empire of rental properties that he'd bought and renovated between 2009 and 2013, while running his car repair shop. I thought of those weekends, during my freshman and sophomore years, when I assisted with renovations or deep cleaning or fumigating the chaos left behind by previous tenants.

Once, Dad and I were repainting the rooms of a duplex, layering coats of a dull beige that matched the quarry tile Mom had found on sale—a shade approximating the color of shit. It was the last item on the agenda before the new tenants moved in, and the easiest, which was why my parents had summoned me from college; I was, of course, useless for the hard-core repairs, which Dad completed on his own. So, we were gripping the poles of our rollers to stay in control and avoid splattering paint. The blisters on our palms—mine from creating art, his from fixing cars at his shop—had burned and throbbed from the start. After a few hours, when our arms had tired from rolling strips of beige, up and down and sidewise, into four-foot squares on the walls (a precise method my custodian uncle had taught us), Dad waved for us to take a break. He dropped his roller, wiped the sweat off his forehead, and slapped my back.

Finally, he said, your Stanford education is useful for us. How wonderful, the implication being, that you could fail your coding classes and learn how to paint for us. He howled, the sound reverberating through my thoughts. Dad had always been the guy who laughed the hardest at his own jokes.

II.
AN EXPLANATION OF DAD,
AS RETOLD BY MOM

Your father missed your birth, Mom said, as she had many times before. (As she will continue saying until she dies or some genius cracks the physics of time travel so that Dad can dodge this mistake and Mom can tell a different story at dinners to explain the dumb shit her husband has done, still does, will always do.) Your father wasn't at the hospital for your birth, and he wasn't there for your sister's, and you want to know why I'm starting this conversation, don't you? Mom directed her fork at me. My son's so entitled, she seemed to be saying, he doesn't deserve the truth I'm dishing out, any more than the veggie stir-fry I made.

Her tone was casual and deadpan despite the rapid pace of her speech; she was as comfortable with life-or-death situations as she was with evading her mother-in-law's weekly inquisitions on whether she could move into the spare room of our new house, which was decorated with paintings of nineteenth-century Nantucket whaling ships that my parents had bought at auction but looked like they came from Costco. Of course, Mom had spent her adolescence slaving away in the rice fields, so nothing really fazed her.

I was in my final months of high school at the time, and felt obnoxiously young and restless, yet wise enough, having got into Stanford with application essays that dredged up my parents' traumatic history in Cambodia as though it were mine. You're telling me, I said, that Ba's always absent. Gone working, what's new? I used my own fork to drag Chinese broccoli, fried tofu, cold rice through a pool of oyster and soy and fish sauces. My stomach was full because I had lately started to eat carne asada burritos stuffed with French fries after my AP classes and before my gig tutoring first-graders for the district.

No, she said, and then sighed. The point: I have zero photos of the first time I held my children.

How was Ba not there? I asked, feeding Mom the same conversational beats, curious to explore her newfound direction for this aging story. Ba was with you when your water broke, right?

When I went into labor, your father dropped me off at the hospital and then drove home to take a shower. He abandoned me for hot water! Every mother in this country, they have touching pictures of meeting their babies. Your father took that away from me. From my children and future grandchildren. When he finally appeared at my bedside, you were already born, she said, her voice hurtling into a scoff of disgust.

It should be stated: Mom has warped many of Dad's actions into war crimes. She developed her gift, I imagine, after the Khmer Rouge genocide, like the Fantastic Four gaining their superpowers from the cosmic rays that sent their spaceship crashing down to earth. Only, in this scenario the rays signify Pol Pot's totalitarian regime; the faulty spaceship evokes Cambodian life under the unstable, short-lived Khmer Republic; and Mr. Fantastic—that rubbery hero overstretching his limbs to fix the deformities of his loved ones, to reach some future in which humanity isn't doomed—stands in for Dad. Meanwhile, fading into the role of sustaining our household, along with holding a full-time job that provided us with health insurance, was Mom, her invisibility a force field refracting her view of the past through the illuminations of her racing thoughts. I didn't know if I'd prefer my proxy to be the Thing or the Human Torch, but since my older sister had been explosive and temperamental as a teenager, my proxy was, I guess, obvious.

I looked at the helm-shaped clock (also bought at auction) as Mom started to peel a persimmon. It's almost ten, I said. The time surprised me and didn't. When Dad secured the loans for his final rental property, he had said, All my hours when I retire I will devote to the duplexes. No more fixing cars at the shop six days a week. The duplexes, my true babies, they will be my life and joy. They never talk back to me. Not like you!

So you are defining retirement as working one full-time job and not two? I asked.

His laugh lines collapsing, folding on top of one another, Dad grinned widely, as if to say, My son can't imagine how much cruelty exists within a point on the grid of our lives, under a patch of our own backyard, just waiting for some idiot, some lazy fool, to trip an explosion.

As Mom ate her persimmon, all I could see around us was flashy junk. Bronze elephants and wooden Apsaras and marble Grecian idols—which no one in our family could identify—crowded every ledge. A sixty-inch TV, perfectly flat, with HD and plasma display, hung over a fireplace Mom had declared was too fancy to hold burning logs. In the corner was a large chair fit to be the throne of a king or a dictator or a masochist who enjoys cramps. Back in the

1980s, Dad and Mom had taken remedial English classes at San Joaquin Delta College (what he later called UBT: the University Behind Target). Sitting next to Mom, copying her answers on grammar and vocabulary quizzes, Dad must have thought, during one lesson, How is less *more*? This teacher believes I have shit for a brain. More is more! Then, later that same day, sporting gold aviators (his favorite style of sunglasses), Dad would have walked into the evening chill, trying to catch the sunset he'd already missed because of his duties at the Sharpe Army Depot—his first job in the U.S.—where, to pay the UBT tuition, he cleaned the floors of the military base, the bathrooms, and the kind of equipment that had been deployed by the soldiers who carpet-bombed his homeland, aggravating the political instability that led to civil war and the Khmer Rouge itself.

After I left home for college, Mom and I would talk on the phone and complain about Dad, his compulsion to work sixteen-hour days, how ridiculous it was for a genocide survivor to be obsessed with accumulating piles of knickknacks. Your husband's getting duped by the so-called American Dream, I'd rant to Mom. CEOs and marketing executives and, like, the whole of capitalism have inducted him into the cult of consumerism, you know, that upholds the worshipping of excessive materialism, the veneration of products, that no one, especially Ba—a goddam Buddhist!—even needs. Though maybe I was too critical and pretentious and hard on Dad. Maybe he harbored some deeper impulse that caused him to grind his hours away.

Maybe, just before my birth, Dad stood in the hospital room, staring at Mom in labor. She would have been sweating and panting through an acute pain inexplicable to him. There he would have been, in his blue-striped work shirt, covered in Mobil 5W-30 oil and maybe the spit of angry customers who had been yelling at him, trained—as he was—to know when a mechanic was scamming them. Glancing down at his forever grease-stained hands, perhaps Dad was thinking, My God, how embarrassing and shitty my life continues to be. One of us, at least, needs to look presentable for our son.

III.
LIKE DIANE ARBUS
BUT WITH CALIFORNIA DUPLEXES

I was riding in the passenger seat, on a mission to document my family's rental properties. Three years into my undergraduate education, I had moved on from an extended, tedious, and shameful period of retaking the computer science classes I'd failed as a freshman. Finally, I was firmly settled in my new major. I'd forged solid relationships with Stanford's art and art history professors, and had even secured a grant that partially funded my materials. I could describe in detail the stunts and creations of, say, Larry Clark or Diane Arbus—their gritty black-and-white photography, their subversive and marginalized subject matter, how their inner lives were inextricably bound with the way their bodies of work would be interpreted after their deaths. I wished to evoke their spirits, to imbue my process with so much novel individuality that artist and aesthetic, intention and creation, would coalesce into my own brand of genius.

In my lap was a Mamiya C220 I'd scored from eBay, which I could afford because of my job as a lab assistant in the Stanford darkroom, and also because I sold weed to other élite stoners. It was akin to the medium-format model Arbus had used. She would level the camera at her waist and then peer into its gaping top to check her framing in the viewfinder, the square reflection caught by that twin lens reflex, before adjusting to an ideal aperture and shutter speed and sealing the picture onto 120 film. Supposedly, the point of my mission was to take photos of Dad's nine duplexes. But I was distracted, all nerves. I was afraid that Dad would sniff out the Mamiya's price tag of three hundred dollars, the Kodak color film that cost fifty dollars a pack, and then some paper trail that would expose my peddling of gateway drugs.

For decades, Dad and Mom had ruthlessly saved money, seeing in our family's future only their own history repeated. This was terrifying, in particular, to Dad. Sometime between his immigration as a penniless refugee in 1981, two years after the fall of Pol Pot, and his naturalization as a U.S. citizen in 1992, the year I was born, Dad had missed his chance to transition out of a bonkers and unsustainable mode of vigilant survival. He buried his money in multiple bank accounts, various secure locations, all around Stockton. In the event of a new regime yanking the rug of basic human needs out from under his feet, Dad would be well prepared. His philosophy—the mantra he recited whenever I had committed any mistake, slight or grand, like my violation of Stanford's academic honor code, for one—was that you could never really be too careful.

Then the 2008 housing crash eliminated jobs and businesses in Stockton, decimating tax revenue and escalating the city's budget crisis. Apparently, the fiscal incompetence of our local politicians and bureaucrats had been laughable, seriously bad—decades of overpromised pensions, a multimillion-dollar project to rebuild the waterfront district (which resulted chiefly in an IMAX movie theater that Dad always refused to go to because of downtown's rate of violent crimes). Soon after the crash, Stockton was deemed the foreclosure capital of the U.S. In 2011, *Forbes* ranked my home town as the most miserable of North American cities. The next year, its government and its lawyers filed for chapter 9 bankruptcy. Naturally, in the aftermath of the Great Recession, Dad capitalized on every opportunity to invest. He poured his life savings into cheap repossessed concrete and started working those sixteen-hour days, Monday through Sunday.

You wanna redo the tile for the duplexes? Dad asked, as he always did when I visited home, or whenever he tried to FaceTime and I instantly pressed Decline and then returned his call without the video interface. (Other things he bothered me about: when I would move home to Stockton and start teaching at UBT, because, you know, I have that shared generational trauma with a Cambodian health instructor on its faculty, and why I had never befriended Andrew Luck, the former quarterback of the Indianapolis Colts, when we overlapped at Stanford. Dad considered the latter the most egregious of my transgressions, worse than my official suspension for an academic quarter—the punishment I earned for plagiarism in a systems programming course.

The same form of disciplinary action Stanford administrators had imposed on a guy in my graduating class after finding him guilty of sexual assault.)

How do your duplexes already need retiling? I answered. Like, isn't quarry tile a decade-long investment?

Dad grunted. You don't do tile for Ba, he said. You can't change the oil of your own car. Can you even climb into walls and fix electrical wiring? You will regret not knowing my skills. One day—when you own a house, when you have a wife (he insisted, even though I'm gay) and kids, after you realize how much you want what your elders have wanted for you and our survival—you'll regret not learning the methods, the tricks, the art of renovation: what Ba tried teaching his youngest, his son. That last part, I assumed, Dad also wanted me to believe.

I laughed and said nothing as we passed the Home Depot where I had spent so many school nights; where I'd stressed over college applications while Mom opened yet another store credit card for the initial discounts; where Dad and I had loaded appliances and supplies into the bed of his Mazda. Freezers and refrigerators. Rolls of carpet and hardwood cabinets. Gas stoves and vented range hoods and bargain countertops. Plus the cases and cases of heavy tile.

The first duplex we visited was in a neighborhood I knew well. The street was by the tae kwon do school my sister and I had attended for years. It was also where my cousins had lived before they moved to West Stockton, to a gated community off the Delta levee, in the kind of suburb to which my parents, too, relocated our household, when Dad's car shop began turning a profit.

We parked across the street. The tenants on the right are gone, Dad said. Ask the family on the left if you can go inside, but don't embarrass me. The adults of the family—two parents, a great-aunt, an uncle without his own wife and kids—were friends of Dad and Mom. They loved my parents for providing them with affordable housing that stayed below market because Dad refused Mom's appeals to hire contractors, repairmen, a superintendent, anyone who might help with the upkeep of the renovated kitchen and bathrooms decked out in granite. All the luxuries Dad had wanted himself. They were also Khmer, like our other tenants, like us. Like my parents and aunts and uncles and oldest cousins and grandmothers, they had survived the Khmer Rouge regime.

Under the dictates of Pol Pot's Khmer nationalism, his false and immoral take on Marxist-Leninist communism, both my grandfathers were potential targets in the first sweep of killings—my Gong on Dad's side had been a schoolteacher, and my Gong on Mom's had owned and operated a rice-processing factory. Their professions had fallen prey to the authoritarian decree of rebooting Cambodia—its society, history, culture—to "Year Zero." In the labor camps, my Gongs kept their heads down, worked in the rice fields with diligence, groveled at the feet of soldiers when necessary, but their obedience resulted only in two extra years of life for each man.

So, the thought of entering the duplex filled me with anxious energy. It felt wrong, as if I'd be crossing a threshold into a parallel universe. I told Dad that I wanted photos of the duplex's exterior, a simple portrait, really, and just that. He shrugged, exiting the truck; the side gate needed fixing, Mom had told him that morning. I stayed in the passenger seat and tinkered with my camera's knobs and dials. The exposure, the depth of field of my twin lens, its focus, I kept resetting.

The reason I had acquired a Mamiya C220 was this: By using a camera that had to be held at one's midsection, Diane Arbus was able to develop a more personal connection with her subjects (or so critics and art historians have argued, even if Susan Sontag found her sensibility less than sympathetic). They could see Arbus's face as she took their photos without peeking through an eyehole, and this lack of a boundary—between subject and artist, the marginalized and the privileged—had the benefit of alleviating the discomfort of posing, of lending out a permanent copy of your image, body, and self, regardless of how society might have made you consider your appearance. I thought that using Arbus's method would best capture the duplexes, that hiding my face behind a camera would be a cop-out.

The sky was cloudless and vast, with infinite gradations. As I stepped out of Dad's truck, the neighborhood and its rocky pavement appeared to me as the floor of an ocean. I looked down into my wide-open viewfinder, at the reflection of the duplex, calibrating the settings to capture the bright austerity in front of me. Steadying the camera, I paused, slowed my breath—I always doubted my initial compositions, as my visual sense was far from being able to grasp what the hell Henri Cartier-Bresson had meant by *decisive* moments. Then I snapped my portrait.

IV.
TRIPTYCH OF RICE PAPER, "PROPERTY BROTHERS," AND LSD

The third time I dropped LSD, I'd just completed an art history exam for a class taught by a professor who happened to be, uncannily enough, Diane Arbus's nephew. Two hundred paintings—their titles and artistic periods, zoomed-in details of their white-gloved hands and royal puppies and grotesque cherubs—still flashed in my brain as my friend and I placed silly tabs on our tongues, *Einstein on the Beach* blasting from my hand-me-down speakers. My friend watched me scroll through a PowerPoint on my laptop, a study guide of all the artworks I had memorized.

Reaching the British Enlightenment, I read out loud my notes on Joseph Wright of Derby, butchering my professor's argument that Wright's early candlelit paintings had served as rough drafts of *An Experiment on a Bird in the Air Pump*. When I finished, my friend and I stared at Wright's paintings, the delicate dark shadows bathed in glowing light, the ominous softness of faces waiting for the demise of a trapped bird, for the end of nature when confronted by the possibilities of knowledge. I turned to my friend and realized he was weeping. I don't know if my friend wept because Wright's conceptual progression had moved him or simply because he felt tortured by my pretentious presence. All I know is that the sight of my weeping friend, the absurdity of our current condition, steered me into panic.

Sitting in my friend's tiny dorm room, immobilized, I thought about how frivolous and offensive my life was. How

Dad worked day and night to put me through Stanford so that I could fail my computer classes and then study art. So I could drop acid on a Tuesday afternoon and sit with my friend who wasted tears on searchable digital images of art. I stared at my hands, and Dad's hands came to me in a vision. Their roughness. The way the calluses made you feel the years of working the rice fields, the decades of repairing cars, the continuous present of duplex renovations. I brought my palms together and let my fingers collapse into themselves. Here were my stupid hands, sheltered from real work. I should use my hands to immortalize the hands of Dad, I thought. I should photograph the duplexes for future generations to see. That's the very least I could do.

Six months later, after developing the film I'd used for the duplex photos, I felt nowhere close to producing art worthy of Dad's labor. The photos were too bare, too simple. I wanted to abandon my drug-induced artistic goal of honoring Dad, retreat to my Stanford dorm, and watch reruns of *Property Brothers*. Instead, I started adding layers of print transfers and wallpaper glue onto the faces of the duplexes. I needed to make portraits that were heartbreaking and scrolls that screamed multiple meanings and collages that would blow everyone's mind. I needed to be great, worthy of the Western canon, of Dad.

A year after taking the duplex photos, I was standing in the lobby of Stanford's art building, which the Great Stanford Investor Gods later tore down. I was installing my senior art show, the culmination of my work, in the hope that my four art professors would bother to look at the giant wall on their way to the building's bathroom. At the center of the wall, I hung huge portraits of Mom, Pol Pot, and Dad, in that order. These were made on Japanese rice paper and collaged together with colorful print transfers. Tiny Khmer Rouge images were layered over one another to form and color in my parents' faces, and these were juxtaposed against a black-and-white pattern of the duplexes. Pol Pot's face, composed only of the duplexes, was an inversion of my parents'. Nearby was a collection of comics I had drawn, many of them featuring Dad. Bookending the exhibit was a pair of giant scrolls made of family photos, more Khmer Rouge images, and wallpaper glue.

I wanted my exhibit to encapsulate everything my parents represented. The portraits' triptych formation was supposed to represent how my parents were haunted by Pol Pot, how, in some skewed perspective on the universe, they almost felt indebted to him for jump-starting their dreams of America. Still, after I hung that last piece and stepped back, what I saw before me didn't feel complete. Worse, it felt compromised. I realized then how much I'd wanted my artworks to reek of my own labor. I'd wanted to imagine that the effort I put into art could match the effort Dad put into the duplexes. Maybe this is why I'm now embarrassed by the oversized portraits and scrolls, those artworks I labored over, the ones I made hopped up on wintergreen oil fumes and wallpaper glue.

V.
ALL OUR SHIT-COLORED TILE

Taking the duplex photographs was about surfaces. It wasn't about illuminating hidden depths, and I can see why a younger version of myself would overcompensate for the photos' simplicity. I had grown up hearing the stories of the genocide, worked to help build our new American identities, and mourned, alongside everyone else in my family, the gaps in our history that could never be recovered. No detail in the duplex photographs stands out. Nothing lends itself to metaphorical thinking. And yet, for me and my family, the duplexes represent the culmination of our history. For anyone else, they mean nothing.

In 1971, Diane Arbus gave a lecture and said, "My favorite thing is to go where I've never been. For me there's something about just going into somebody else's house." I've imagined Diane Arbus saying this to me in a conversation. In my head, we are at some café and having tea, just tea, because I can't see Diane eating much. An acute intensity ripples out of the angles of her limbs and cropped hair. Diane explains to me her fascination with the people she photographed, the lives she documented, all the things she's learned about the underbelly of humanity over the years. I ask her how she accounts for the gap between the complexity of her subjects and the reductive quality of a photograph. She responds to me with her other famous quote: "Lately I've been struck with how I really love what you can't see in a photograph."

Then Diane asks me about my own house, and I tell her about the duplexes. I say, I think of roaches, endless waves of roaches washing across the tile. They creep out of the crevices of every sticky cupboard.

I remember trying to clean, with off-brand bleach wipes, the mountains of filth left in the duplexes when a tenant moved out, which happened a lot in Stockton's bankrupt economy. Moldy food fermented into entire ecosystems of bacteria. Mysterious stains everywhere, even, I swear, speckling the ceilings. Dust caked into the carpets so thoroughly that every step through a room raised a cloud of particulate matter, a storm of skin flakes.

I remember Mom complaining once about the tenants' fucking up the duplex so much that her vacuum broke sucking up all the filth. She's wearing a safety mask, like Dad, like my sister, and like me, because Dad has had to set off poison bombs to kill the roaches. You owe me a new vacuum, Mom says to Dad, making it known in the cadence of her voice, even through the mask, that she never signed up for this shit.

Halfway through cleaning the duplex, we gather in the living room. Each of us squats on a different object not meant to be a chair—a cooler, a toolbox, a stack of spare tile—except Mom, who brings in a lawn chair and reminds us, again, without saying a word, that she's not dealing with any extra, unnecessary discomfort. After this, I'm getting a massage, Mom mutters under her breath, but still loud enough that we—most important, Dad—hear her.

Homemade sandwiches of roasted pork, pâté, and pickled daikon get passed around, and so does a single water bottle we all share. I used to hate your father, Mom says, signaling for the communal bottle. When he led us through the mines in the forest for the second time, because the first time armed Thai soldiers at the border ordered us to turn back, your father was freaking insensitive to me.

So, he was an asshole, I say, which prompts Mom to slap my arm for being disrespectful.

I was so thirsty, Mom continues, I thought I would die of

dehydration. And your father, he had two whole containers of water. He drank from one, and he poured the other over his face because he was hot. Can you imagine? The rest of us are dying of thirst, and your father keeps pouring water on himself, like he needs to take a shower in the middle of a forest.

Dad starts cracking up and takes a bite of his sandwich. Don't listen to her, Dad says, his mouth full of pâté. Your mother was a rich girl, and she thought someone would just give her water even though she never asked for it. You guys are all so rich, Dad says, pointing the remainder of his sandwich at us accusingly. You're barely Cambodian. You're barely Cambodian-American! Just remember, he adds, remember where you came from. We watch as he spreads his arms out wide. For a brief moment, we believe his wingspan can encompass the entirety of the duplexes, maybe even more.

If I could resurrect the hungry ghost of Diane Arbus, I would show her the duplex photos hanging on my wall, three thousand miles away from Stockton. I'd tell Diane all about the tile Dad has laid with his bare hands, the foundation he cemented in grout for our sparkling new lives, how no one in our family will touch that tile with their bare feet. How we'll never feel that morning coldness jolting our tired bodies into waking life.

"We stand on a precipice," Diane wrote on a postcard in 1959, years before her suicide. "Then before a chasm, and as we wait it becomes higher, wider, deeper, but I am crazy enough to think it doesn't matter which way we leap because when we leap we will have learned to fly."

A YEAR IN READING

NONFICTION, ORIGINALLY PUBLISHED
IN *THE MILLIONS*

This year I have started almost a hundred books and finished none of them. It's not a terrible way to live as a writer with political and aesthetic aims of the lofty, masochistic variety, whose first novel draft will definitely push the limits of digestible length. Call it reading not as binge-worthy commitment, not proof of literary engagement—indulgent showboating, at its worst—but instead as a mode of aesthetic encountering. I actually recommend everyone to stop taking books so seriously, so monogamously, as though the price of hardcovers were only justified through the number of titles logged into Goodreads. Never have I been more productive as a lover of prose.

Before I continue, I do want to say: maybe not entirely my fault! I did attend a crowded public high school where teachers assigned few novels or full-length plays a year. During sophomore year, my English class spent two months on *The Great Gatsby* but never chewed on the tragic death of its eponymous schmuck, as the library recalled our copies to give to another class of forty students. (Our teacher, making up for this glaring hole in our Western cultural education, later devoted a week's worth of instruction to watching the 1974 film adaptation; somehow, our class was denied, yet again, the epiphanic experience of F. Scott Fitzgerald's ending, however diluted by David Merrick's sterile and wack direction. The next semester our teacher resigned herself to sending our class off into the "SSR" woods, as in "silent sustained reading." As in the educational cornerstone of elementary language arts, of second-graders learning to concentrate and sit frozen with stoic obedience.) Even my AP Literature seminar of college-bound seniors focused on just two books: *Hamlet* and *Invisible Man*. While I remember this teacher somewhat fondly, she was not equipped to riff on Black characters and the failures of white-centered Marxism.

And before I self-incriminate any further: I swear (as a courtesy to my editor and agent and public-facing persona, as well as the privacy of my literary group chats, not to forget the boyfriend who hates how far-reaching my dumb, petty mouth often stretches), truly, emphatically, that these past months of noncommittal reading have little to do with hot takes on [the] Big Four publishing conglomerates. Or the nihilism of overeducated, philosophy queer bros I sometimes, unfortunately, find myself guilty of affecting.

Anyway, it's true! My mushy quarantine brain has been commandeered by a fuck-boy approach to literature. I remain incapable of finishing novels and poetry collections, memoirs and nonfiction books and academic monographs, or, at my most scattered, single short stories, even those written by dear friends. At any given moment, thirty to fifty tabs—usually the preview pages of books I've marked to buy or borrow from the library, which land on my radar at the recommendation of peers and mentors whose literary tastes I adore—are left open in Google Chrome for weeks on end, maybe months. I also sabotaged four book clubs, one of them organized by yours truly.

Through a number of these books, I made a not insignificant, not not respectable headway, having consumed a chunk of their words before dropping their characters and speakers like I did the majority of my high school graduating class—with zero notions of ill will. Hopefully, someday, I will finish every book I started. Perhaps when I write the ending to my novel. While tinkering with my opening pages, I read so many first pages while stoned in my neighborhood bookstore. Several weeks later, when I got stranded in the gulf between chapters two and three, I proceeded to the next fifty pages of half of these same books. Each time my dialogue comes out stilted, I read bangers from *The Collected Poems of Frank O'Hara*. All I want is for my characters to speak like Frank O'Hara.

To formulate my novel's voice, the narrator's range of telling, I hopped through Friedrich Nietzsche's *The Gay Science*, Danez Smith's *Homie*, James McBride's *Deacon King Kong*. Its structure: I got a third of the way into those collected interviews of Roberto Bolaño's *The Savage Detectives*. Its ancestors: a combined thirty pages of Ludovico Ariosto's *Orlando Furioso* and Henry Fielding's *The History of Tom Jones*, before I realized how hopeless it was to locate heirs for my stoner novel about queer Khmer Americans. Might as well be my own daddy.

Okay, I misrepresented. I trekked to the endings of a few novels. Right as I was passing the ten-year mark for my high school graduation, I reread *Invisible Man* and finally understood just how little I had learned in AP Literature. How the fuck did I miss so much of Ellison's genius? I asked myself, overwhelmed by this epic I've always thought to be a favorite of mine. I guess understanding has nothing on profound impact.

Then I read *The Adventures of Augie March*, by Saul Bellow. It's absurd to me that I've cast aside dozens of novels and somehow finished two dense behemoths. Maybe I just vibe with lost narrators full of hope. Like Ellison's narrator, I want to believe that "when I discover who I am, I'll be free." Like Augie, I haplessly take wisdom from those who cannot guide me. Too bad over 1.5 million people died in the Cambodian genocide.

I did love *Girl, Woman, Other*, by Bernardine Evaristo. Or maybe I loved knowing the characters of this kaleidoscopic novel. Maybe I need to record the lives of as many archetypal Khmer queers as I can imagine.

I should return to the books I have yet to finish! The first story of David Means's collection *Instructions for a Funeral*, "Fistfight, Sacramento, August 1950," dazzled me with its slow, hypnotic recursion, its dilation of time that ebbs and flows with every sucker punch, every decline and uptick of glorious, pathetic testosterone. I don't understand how others can so easily open this collection without spending all their time basking, cheering, stepping inside those fighting passages. And I felt a similar sensation, this devotion for swaggering, cocky syntax, while immersed within *Luster*. That breathless account of delivery gigs and mishaps, it dead-ass bullied me into dropping Raven Leilani's debut novel and working on my own. I was slapped by that whirlwind of manic energy and meaning-making the protagonist, Edie, conveys from one drop-off spot to the next until she slams hard against the guarded stony walls of her fuck buddy.

Speaking of sentences, I'm stuck on the first line of Sarah M. Broom's *The Yellow House*. I'm a lovesick idiot. I can't break from this absurd romantic loop. The cosmic movement from aerial shots to the home address that Broom knows best—that "scab of green" where her brother Rabbit, her brother Carl, can be found sitting "poised on an ice chest," this lone man of two names always searching and fishing for wonder—was enough to plant the seeds of my own essay collection that's now already germinating.

I admit I am a selfish reader. I consume literature for the sustenance of my own writing. Maybe I should be more respectful of these stories and their authors and take them all on their own terms of understanding. I should lock my feet into those proverbial shoes of others not myself the way my sophomore English teacher, for the betterment of our society, dictated my class to do.

Still, I've always thought of total empathy as overrated. That it teaches one to care, sure, but never to build intimacy that accommodates for unknowability. At least not without bleaching nuance with bloated universal ideas. Plus, I try not to befriend those who seek listeners and nothing else—

not collaborators, not intellectual and cultural exchange—because I love dialogue! How awesome to witness Sigrid Nunez match the genius of *The Friend* with *What Are You Going Through?* Thank god Nunez granted her narrator the freedom of generous interiority, emotional responses, visceral thinking. Pretty sadistic if the narrator were forced to comfort a dying, suicidal friend with her inner voice gagged and duct-taped into silence.

Fuck, what the hell do I know? I've been on page 130 for months. Of course—I hate to say—that didn't stop me from praising this novel to everyone I could.

THE ROSES

FICTION, FROM *STRAIGHT THRU CAMBOTOWN*

They say Visith Ros, known as Pou Sith, the owner of Mekong Jewelry, was a cold-hearted father, his droopy face creased with lines like crooked canals meant to drain his large, sullen eyes of life. He cracked nonstop jokes and laughed with everyone except those closest to him, such as his family, with whom he was so bitterly serious as to be himself a joke. He hated America but loved everything about being an American citizen. He loved, for instance, the easy access to the internet, how he could stream Khmer music from YouTube whenever he wanted, even from his phone. He loved driving on freeways, marveled at those concrete roads twisting through mountains and across deserts, and even sitting in bumper-to-bumper traffic he found worthwhile, as he'd watch that slow procession of every possible car, of every color and size, one could own and drive.

It was this panoply of choices he loved most about America. But as much as Pou Sith loved his citizenship—as sure as he was that he'd never return to Cambodia for good, unlike his sister-in-law's cowardly ex-husband (who had burdened Pou Sith with his wife and son to support and feed for a decade), and unlike so many of his friends, really—he would never forgive America for one indelible transgression.

When Pou Sith first stepped into that U.S. immigration processing center in the Philippines, after living in the refugee camps of Thailand for over a year, his malnourished body was swollen with hope. He had nothing to his name, nothing beyond the damage inflicted upon his life, the imprinting of war, death, starvation, labor, and torture that had accumulated beneath his skin, and while he waited in that impossibly crowded line, everything he had endured flashed through his consciousness, an unrelenting reel of tragedy. So, he did what he always did when the past was threatening to overwhelm his mind, his body, to the point of collapse; he named all the people in his life who'd died.

His mother. His father. His grandparents. His older brother. His older brother's wife and two infants. His younger brother and their two best friends. Then eight of his cousins and twenty of his second cousins and even more of his second cousins' children. And so on. All these people's lives were sacrificed so he could be standing here, under this oversized tent propped up by the U.S. Army. Their pain and memories fueled the hope that maybe his suffering would finally come to an end. He muttered their names under his breath, raindrops leaking from the tent's roof, battering his head. When he ran out of names, he started over from the beginning.

His wife, Chhorwon, was too busy comforting her

younger sisters, Nary and Peou, to hear his muttering. They stood ahead of him, their arms intertwined, forming a barrier between those who preceded them and those behind. Chhorwon told her sisters not to worry, that if they made it through this last stop, they would be reunited with their mother, who was already settled in California.

Even though the U.S. officials had promised that everyone would be processed through immigration, the humid air in the tent was charged with anxiety, with desperation. A company of soldiers guarded the perimeter of the tent, armed with rifles and ready to fire at the crowd—these brown bodies more or less indistinguishable, to them, from those they'd been trained to see as the enemy.

And then Pou Sith and his family were at the front of the line. His wife's youngest sister was talking to the officers sitting at a table covered with stacks and stacks of paper.

"Ma'am, who else are you with here?" an officer yelled, and then another officer yelled the same thing, but in a broken, halting Khmer.

Peou didn't say anything, and the two officers kept yelling at her, one in English and the other in Khmer, a cacophony of language, until Peou pointed at her two sisters and then Pou Sith, saying their first names. And just like that, it happened, with a swift stamp and some bureaucratic scribbling, Pou Sith was adorned with his wife's surname. His father's name was denied entry into America. Officially, on this day, as he stood in a country he had never lived in and would never revisit, he became "Visith Ros."

This was why Pou Sith had hated America—it had erased his name from history.

Over the years, of course, he thought about legally changing his name back to its original form. But there were always too many hours to work, too many children to support, and his wife refused to take part in this initiative, dreading the hassle of changing all the tax documents, the rental leases, and then notifying her children's schools and so on. Even when the burden of life eased and he opened his own business and this business started turning a profit, Pou Sith found reasons to delay that trip to the courthouse. At first he thought, *When I stop having kids, then I'll do it.* Then he thought he'd wait until his eldest was old enough to appreciate the symbolic value of father and son, together, changing their names back to that birthright. What a grand day that would be, their reclaiming of patrilineal honor.

But by the time Vinny had hit puberty, though, every time Pou Sith so much as mentioned that "Ros" wasn't their true last name, his son would respond with something like "Ba, why do we have to change our names? I got a good thing going on here. Vinny Ros—that's the name of a famous person, yo? There's a ring to it. Can't mess with a good thing. My name's got momentum. You know? Potential."

And Molly would add, "Why does only Vinny get to have a new last name?!"

"Let's all go change our names, then," Pou Sith would say.

"No, I don't want to change my name, either," Molly inevitably snapped. "Especially since clearly you don't even care about me, your daughter, having your last name."

Then Pou Sith would drop the whole conversation, delaying his reclamation of his name, his lineage, his goddamn manhood, just a bit longer. He was always delaying, Pou

Sith; everything he delayed, from paying off his loans to the Circle of Money (being the brother-in-law of the Counter did have its benefits) to telling his children he was proud of their accomplishments (back when they still had worthy accomplishments, that is, such as winning basketball games or earning good grades) to playing a winning sequence before it was too late during the weekly Big Two poker nights he attended with other disgruntled, emasculated Cambo husbands and fathers. And now, right when he had just started to let go of the past, let go of his resentment, his children had suddenly become adults, and he sometimes could hardly recognize them. They were mutated now, had transformed irrevocably in their years away from Cambotown, their skin now inked and stained, their postures in perpetual defiance of his authority. He couldn't help but think that his children's refusal to snap themselves into place, to do something worthwhile with their lives, instead of pursuing the paths of deadbeat artist and criminal rapper, was a direct consequence of their false names, and now that his two children were back at home, living under the same roof again (at least for the next few weeks), he had begun to think that his past resentment was always misdirected.

It was never America that was his undoing, never America that had precipitated the decline of his children; no, their being born in America was the very thing that had given them all the opportunities in the world, opportunities they had spent the last decade wasting. Rather, it was the person who had given America the wrong name. To Pou Sith, then, Peou was the reason his children Vinny and Molly had become the failures they were.

THAT RICH BITCH, POU SITH thought the morning of the Peou's funeral, furious that he had to close Mekong Jewelry for the day, to say nothing of having been subjected to his wife's agitated ravings all week, the utter pandemonium that had ruffled the whole town because of one death. And what was one death in the face of so many deaths that had already befallen them? He sat at the wobbly card table tucked away in the back corner of the kitchen, which he loved because, seating only one person comfortably, it discouraged his family members from disrupting his morning routine. He and Ming Won had acquired it, for free, from the local Episcopal church when they first immigrated. (A note on Christianity in Cambotown: Back in the '80s, different Christian sects tried converting refugee families, offering social services and free stuff, including furniture, in an attempt to recruit more church members. Cambos being devoutly attached to their Buddhist roots—their stubborn worship of karma and reincarnation having endured French colonialism for decades—this evangelizing succeeded mostly in Cambos' taking advantage of poor Christian white folk, taking any- and everything they offered, before they returned to their own observances.)

As he did every morning, Pou Sith was reading the real estate section of the *Press-Telegram*, fantasizing about the houses he could buy under his true name, while drinking black coffee and eating a bowl of Honey Bunches of Oats doused in Yeo's soybean drink. The morning sunlight flooded the kitchen with an aggressive glow, or maybe it just appeared that way because Ming Won, still miffed about the

Lort Guy, was Saran Wrapping trays of stir-fried glass noodles with what seemed unnecessary force.

"I've been leaving voice mails for him all week," she said, stretching the cling wrap from its giant roll. The plastic screech was so obnoxious it forced Pou Sith to push his newspaper away. "I remember that boy in diapers," she continued, "have been buying his lort for years, and now he won't answer my calls."

"Stop this," Pou Sith said in that clipped voice he used with his wife, or anyone he both cared for and belittled. "No one will notice. You already have too much food."

"That's not the point!"

The evening before, Vinny and Molly had returned home empty-handed from their conquest to find the Lort Guy, and Ming Won instantly knew they were high, could tell from their bloodshot eyes, the paranoid bobs of their heads. Molly had expected Ming Won to snatch and twist their ears, and even Vinny, who'd spent his adolescence and early twenties growing increasingly immune to his parents' lectures about smoking weed, flinched at the sight of their mother's knowing look. The siblings mentally prepared their defenses of what had happened, their recounting of the Lort Guy's mother's inexplicable and visceral reaction toward their presence. Molly even considered mentioning how she saw the Lort Guy hiding in his mother's house, but decided against it, just as she'd decided against telling Vinny and Darren, at least for now, the fact of its feeling so cataclysmic, she wasn't ready to entertain other perspectives.

But Ming Won didn't say anything about their being high. After spending the whole day cooking for the funeral, alongside equally hotheaded women, she simply looked defeated by the sight of these stoned, empty-handed children of hers. Her large, glassy eyes, usually alert and darting, painfully attentive to her surroundings, appeared glazed over. But that was the night before, and now Ming Won had recovered, however briefly, her fierce temperament, that dinging in her head always urging her to plow through whatever needed to be done. And this morning, wearing a silk nightgown, her hair wrapped in a red-and-gold krama scarf, that dinging was feeding her constant cursing of the Lort Guy.

"What do you mean he wasn't at your stupid card game!" Ming Won yelled at Pou Sith. "He's always there!"

"Well, he wasn't this time," Pou Sith said, and Ming Won launched into another diatribe—how the Lort Guy's parents owed her and Peou; without them, their illegitimate dessert business would've never established professional connections with proper Cambo grocery stores.

Pou Sith just nodded. He was busy strategizing how to break it to his children that this week, they would finally change their last names. For all he knew, he would be the next person to die in the family (he had been on the verge of diabetes for the past decade), and then all hope would be lost, his tombstone forever marked with his wife's surname, with no one remembering who he actually was. What more opportune time?—with his children so grief-stricken. And maybe they would even want to do something, anything, to sever their future from their past, to step into a new path with a new name and be able to look back and say, That was the old me.

Plus, he wanted to cut down Peou in some way on her big day, this carnival of grief costing him an entire day's profit.

Molly entered the kitchen and went straight for the coffee pot. "God, you didn't leave me any?"

"Aah, you, I have something I need you to do, once and for all," Pou Sith responded. "Go to the courthouse and change your last name. To your real name."

"Ba, this . . . again?"

"What's happening again?" Vinny said, walking in shirtless and yawning. "Shit, did I miss Ba's coffee? Man, baby sis, I love you, but you can't make coffee for shit."

"If you are going to live under my roof," Pou Sith said, "no questions allowed!"

"Woah, can we all take a chill pill?" Vinny said.

Vinny and Molly stared at their father, bracing themselves for whatever he had to say next. On one side of the kitchen, Molly leaned into the counter ledge while Vinny sat atop the opposite counter, his legs dangling, their respective ribs and butt cheeks so well accustomed to the sharp ledge of that seafoam-green tile. Whenever their parents had lectured them about skipping classes or being rude to elders or hanging with idiot delinquents like Rithy or Kelvin, this was where they positioned themselves. For whatever reason, their nuclear family always congregated here, in the smallest room of the house. There was a dining room with an expensive table crafted of oak, with meticulous decorative carvings along the edges, one of the first purchases Pou Sith and Ming Won had made when upgrading to this second house, but it was always covered with business receipts from the jewelry shop and bundles of incense, candles, and tapioca candies for the various events that Ming Won helped organize. There was also a living room with a large sectional couch, a plasma HD flat-screen television, but it had effectively become Pou Sith's second bedroom as he often fell asleep during football games or *Die Hard* action sequences. So, the cramped kitchen, with its pale fluorescent lighting, its permanent stench of lemongrass and fish sauce, had become the family's core, the place where they discussed any and all pertinent matters.

"It is important for you to change your names," Pou Sith said, "and it is important for you to do it this week."

"Ba, I thought we were past this," Vinny said.

"It doesn't even matter what our names are," Molly added.

"I don't need to explain myself," Pou Sith said. "Just do what I tell you."

"Mai, can you believe this?" Molly asked. She started measuring coffee grounds into a filter, demonstrating her apathy by resuming her morning routine.

"Believe what? You mean that stupid boy?" Ming Won responded, now stacking all the trays on top of each other into a precarious tin tower of food. "Everyone will judge us for not having lort."

"Not saying I'm judging you, Mai, or us as a family unit," Vinny said, "but damn, every good event has lort."

Just then, Pou Sith was about to lecture his kids about the value and legacy of his patrilineal bloodline, how his own father was the most respected man in the village right outside Battambang, not only the principal of the only elementary school but also the history teacher. Generation after generation Pou Sith's father had cultivated into respectable adults, before he was targeted during the regime for being an educator, an arbiter of knowledge of what Cambodia had been in the times preceding Year Zero. Pou Sith saw his father as embodying the very spirit of the Cambodian culture. But before Pou Sith could utter a sound, Ming Won seized the reins of the conversation.

"We don't have time for this! Vinny, Molly—go to the store and buy all the lort you can. As many cups as possible. When you get back, we can pour them all into a big bowl."

"So much plastic, such a waste," Vinny said, before he and Molly shuffled out of the kitchen, dodging their father's scrutiny.

Pou Sith sighed. After so many years of these same conversations that led nowhere, he hardly had the energy to keep fighting, not right now, anyway. But soon, something would give, as Peou was dead, and today they were setting her remains on fire. Soon, Pou Sith thought, things would change; he knew they would. And if things changed enough, then maybe his two idiot children would finally come around to the idea that what they had inherited from him, and not his wife, nor his wife's family, was the source of energy they should have been tapping into their whole lives.

With the Counter of the Circle of Money gone and dead, there would be a massive restructuring of Cambotown society. Pou Sith had seen it before, when he was barely a teenager. His uncle—his father's brother—had been the Counter of their village, but then illness struck him. Yes, Pou Sith could see it all coming here in Cambotown, too. Wealth would be redistributed through the community, even within families, and new powers would form. People would fight their way into the spotlight, form new alliances, and claim what they had decided was theirs all along.

Oh, it would be nothing like the Communists taking over—how the social hierarchy was flipped upside down (except for those secretly always in power who escaped before Pol Pot took over), how the rich and the educated were beaten to the ground by the poor, who had been waiting for the opportunity to make something of their lives. But there was still the risk of some of that. Pou Sith didn't know anything for sure about Peou's tenure as the Counter (only grumblings from his poker night, gossip from his wife, traces he had overheard from Peou's phone calls), but he understood deeply how money twisted knots into a person's thoughts, distorting what appeared as true and what appeared as good. He saw this whenever customers came into his store even though they couldn't yet afford anything, how they looked for glimpses of their own reflections in the sheen and sparkle of those jewels, wanting so badly to enact diamond-studded clichés of status. This was part of the reason Pou Sith's own wife was losing her mind planning this funeral, wasn't it? Pulling it off would be Ming Won's last chance to assert their family's power. She wanted everyone to know that Peou's death meant nothing in terms of their status and strength.

It could be a thankless job, serving as the Counter, holding people accountable to their debts. It often brewed resentment, and he, out of everyone, was aware of the potential toxic feeling seething just beneath the veneer of shared blood, or community, or culture. Pou Sith wouldn't wish it upon anyone, this job, and beyond his own selfish desire for his children to bear his true name, he hoped that soon Vinny and Molly would no longer share Peou's, that their connection to the former Counter would be made as distant as possible, before that building resentment punctured right through the always precarious present.

THE COUSINS AT THE FUNERAL

FICTION, FROM *STRAIGHT THRU CAMBOTOWN*

Tucked into a leafy narrow backstreet, Pacific Mortuary sat on a lot without enough parking, behind a Foods 4 Less—also with inadequate parking—and a boba tea café. But this never stopped them. Not even in our current time are these women ever thwarted.

It was an hour or so before Peou's funeral, scheduled for 1 p.m., and I suspect they parked on Anaheim Street, or maybe at their friend's house on Acacia Street, or maybe their children or grandchildren or kmouys dropped them off. Perhaps they were related to Battambang Bai's owner and leveraged blood and bygone days for access to his spacious concrete. Three decades of deaths had hardened them to the scant parking, the claustrophobic side streets, the high density of bodies per square mile resulting from the largest Cambodian American population being crammed into one midsized section of one midsized Californian city. All this was a necessary function of their free lives. Their neighborhood encompassed an entire universe; naturally, there was no room for ample parking.

The first to arrive for the funeral, the women climbed out of hunks of metal, some of the cars beat up and running since the 1980s, others shiny and gaudy, painted colors such as teal and orange-bronze (the colors nobody actually wanted, forcing salesmen to throw out Hail Mary discounts). All the Mas and Mings and Mais, dressed in white, carrying their signature dishes, formed a blinding procession. There was Ming Vee, with her beef tripe sour soup; Ohm Lee, with her fried fish smothered in shredded green papaya; Ohm Vey, with her glutinous rice logs stuffed with pork belly and mung beans swaddled in banana leaves. Nothing canned or expired for the funeral of the Counter!

And yes, the food was for the monks.

And yes, the monks were for Peou's soul, her rebirth into a new life.

And once the monks were done praying, and once Peou's core family and devoted groupies carried the coffin to the detached building, then the food would be eaten by the monks, and then by everyone else.

But that was scheduled for later, Darren knew, and he wished he harbored zero expectations. He wished he were still a kid again, that he wasn't cursed with the forced maturity of awareness. If he were entirely ignorant of the histrionic shit saddling every Cambotown funeral, maybe he could immerse himself in the warmth of communal grieving. He almost felt cheated.

Darren stood in the mahogany-clad foyer of Pacific Mortuary, next to a giant canvas photo of Peou, fighting the urge to refresh his email. He had already checked his phone ten times in the past thirty minutes, for news on a scholarship application he'd submitted the previous fall, and now he felt like a dickhead. What was PhD news in the face of a beloved relative's death, he'd told himself all week, with some success, until this morning. He felt his guts being churned through the gears of his worry. After the funeral, there would be no more distractions. Sooner or later, he needed to figure out his plans for the next year. Unless . . . he was awarded the scholarship. That would make the decision easy, he assumed, would give him the perfect excuse. It was the most prestigious scholarship for emerging Asian American academics in the country. More important, it would determine his living stipend for the next three years.

Trying to clear his mind, he shook his head, like one would a Magic 8 Ball, and then looked at Peou's large pixelated face. It was a rush job, the canvas portrait, an image cropped from a bigger one, a headshot that stood up to Darren's shoulders. That morning, Ming Nary had sent Darren to print it at Kinkos, right after she forced him to shave his head. The original image had been taken at his tenth birthday party. He was sitting on Peou's lap, a cake topped by lit candles in front of them. The best photo of Peou they had, Ming Nary claimed. Look how pretty your Ming was. She was your second mother.

There Darren was, in an uncomfortable charcoal suit, next to a giant photo he'd been sliced out of, forcibly, unreasonably, by his own mother. *There's a joke in this*, Darren thought, pulling at his sleeves, which still carried that stiff sheen of newness, as Ming Nary had bought this suit for him right before he entered his PhD program. Something good enough for Stanford, she kept saying to the tailor in Nordstrom, before maxing out another credit card.

On the opposite side of Peou's portrait, wrapped in a white sarong and skirt, Ming Nary greeted each Cambo woman carrying food, who all planted sloppy kisses on Darren's cheeks, lips, forehead, even one on his left eye. "Oun, I'm so sorry for your loss. Where should we put this food?"

"Right over there," he repeated, pointing into the main room on his left, down the aisle splitting the pews, toward the stage, where the monks would pray in front of their feast, where Molly would deliver her eulogy.

Maybe I should stay with the monks, he then thought, as he crouched into an embrace with a Ming barely five feet tall, who promptly left into the main room, along with his mother. He scratched his scalp, grazed the prickly edges of his remaining hair. His head was already buzzed, so that part was done. But he felt too old for it to really matter. He was past the age of some youthful teenager who could benefit from a week at the temple. And Peou was his Ming, not his Mai, not his Ma, so no one pressed the issue, not even Ming Won.

Behind Darren and Peou's portrait, a makeshift triptych of three paintings loomed over the foyer. It was installed by the mortuary's owner after the last funeral he'd attended some years ago. The middle image was the largest, twice the width of the other two, and Darren recognized the style to be that of Pieter Bruegel the Elder, the pigments a rustic tint of faded brightness. He couldn't name the exact painting, but he could tell it was a cheap reproduction. Though, he mused, it would be hilarious, wouldn't it? That a priceless Flemish painting might be housed in Cambotown, where biblical allegories fell on deaf Buddhist ears.

Darren scoffed, then examined the paintings more closely.

—

NOW, I'VE TAKEN A GOOD look at this famous Cambotown triptych. I've experienced, through my own eyes, my own flesh, the startling effect it has on a grieving Cambo's spirit. When Darren told me about that morning of the funeral, I knew exactly why he was so struck by those haunting images. I've stood where Darren stood, cranking my neck to peer into those canvases.

The middle painting, the Bruegel, features a partially constructed, slightly askew tower reaching into the sky, its base wider at the bottom, its levels narrowing and narrowing in their ascent. It sits at the shoreline of a blue-green sea that extends to the right edge of the frame. Scaffolding and construction equipment are sporadically placed around the building. The unfinished interior at the top burns a pale red, as though the tower is alive and breathing, its bleeding guts exposed to the air, the collapsed upper-mid level on the right just a healing scab. A growth of rock and earth has almost overtaken the tower's center core. Or is that the spilling of a botched construction now hardened?

In the bottom-left corner, a band of men—some carrying spears, others on the ground begging, praying, worshiping—encircle a bearded leader adorned with a crown, a white robe, an air of nobility from the tips of his golden boots to the edge of his sword. They appear to be strategizing their next steps. The leader has thrust his sword in the direction of the open sea. *Let's venture forth into those mysterious waters!* he seems to be saying. Behind the tower, there lies a city of multicolored homes, and then, farther into the horizon, grassy fields lead to delicate, simple mounds.

Why couldn't they go there? Darren wondered, as I've wondered. *Or even stay where they were?* What was wrong with this clear and reasonable landscape in the shadow of this tower?

Darren now focused on the other two paintings. On the Bruegel reproduction's left side hung a slim portrait of Jesus, long hair flowing down to his waist. On the right: an equally slim portrait of a bodhisattva. Except, something was off, Darren noticed. The Jesus was painted to look Khmer, with dark skin, a broad nose, a face you'd see carved into Angkor Wat. And the bodhisattva—white! Anglo, completely so, with giant blue eyes.

What the fucking shit? he thought, as I've thought, right as the Roses entered the foyer, each of them carrying twice as much food as anyone else. Adorned in traditional clothes, Ming Won and Pou Sith looked as grave as ever, ghostly in their white outfits, and they both headed into the main room. Molly and Vinny shot straight to Darren with the instinctual purpose of fish swimming upstream.

Vinny was dressed in the lightest of gray slacks, sparkling white Air Jordans, and a traditional silk button-down without a collar. Molly wore a floral dress with a sarong draped around her torso. Both Ros siblings mirrored their parents. Even though half the men would be in suits, Darren regretted wearing one, almost wished that the funeral would just take place at the local wat, so that everything was uniform, consistent, logical. But Ming Nary had wanted him to look like an adult, the man of the family.

"And you doubted that we'd get our hands on some lort!" Vinny exclaimed, holding up his silver basin, which was intricately imprinted with Buddhist insignias.

"What're you talking about?" Darren said. "I never doubted shit."

"We really have to talk," Molly said.

"Yeah, bruh, about how you're ripping off my look!" Vinny said, raising his eyebrows to gesture at his own shaved head.

Darren rolled his eyes. "You know this is for the funeral."

"Guys," Molly said, "we have serious shit to discuss!"

"Today is all serious, baby sis. Don't worry."

Just then, Ohm Vey came up to the cousins. "Oh my poor babies!" she exclaimed, forcing Darren into a hug. "You were Ah-Peou's favorites, her jewels, her reason for being alive, for working as hard as she did, for making all her money, for everything, really. She was so proud, of all of you! And wow, Stanford. Just—wow! I can see why she loved you all so much. My own children, they are much older—"

"We know who your kids are," Molly said, clutching her basin of nom lort closer to her chest.

"Oh my own children! How I wish they'd go to business school like you!"

"I'm studying philosophy," Darren said.

"They never were any good at school. They only went to the community college, never even got their AA degrees.

Years I paid their tuitions, and nothing, and what are they doing now? They are bums."

This time, Vinny interrupted: "I thought your son was the manager of the Best Buy."

"If he had a Stanford degree, maybe he would own his own Best Buy!"

All three cousins made a face. *Just-gotta-disengage-but-damn-it's-hard-when-this-lady's-spewing-out-nonsense*, they were expressing through Darren's clenched jaw and Molly's flared nostrils and Vinny's bewildered eyes.

"But you know, I was one of Ah-Peou's closest friends! I'm not sure if Ah-Peou ever—uhm—told you that, but yes, I was very top of the list of friends close to her. I always did right by her! Yes, yes, yes, one time, I remember it so well, very well, she stopped by my house to do her collections and her stomach was hurting, she was in so much pain, and nothing was working. She had coined the skin of her stomach with moongalaw already. Remember how I used to coin your backs until you cried! Funny children, you were to babysit. Anyway, Ah-Peou had even taken Pepto Bismol already, and still—nothing! Can you believe it! She couldn't, I couldn't, no one could! She was moaning in pain, she just could not bear it any longer, and neither could I, because I was experiencing as much pain as she was, just from watching her as she sat on my couch, clutched her stomach, so I went straight to my kitchen and searched through my pantry for anything that would help. Then I remembered what I used to give my children when they were feeling sick. You know, I was the one who figured out a Sprite recipe to cure stomach pain and migraines! It's all in the way you mix it with the medicine. Advil and Sprite, a blessing! Tylenol and 7UP, watch out! I put in a secret ingredient in there, too, of course. Don't trust those other ladies who think they know how to cure pain like I can! You can't just rely only on the American products, and, well, relying on just Cambodian ones? I'm not one of those hags who thinks she's some magical witch from the old times!"

"Ohm," Darren said, "maybe you should go find a seat before it gets too crowded."

"I promise the story is almost done! I know you have Stanford business that keeps you busy. Your Ming Peou—also a businessperson, like you!—she was so grateful for my Sprite healing mix, she forgave my payment for that round of collections. That was how much I helped her. Please, just, if you can, when you think of me, know that I saved Ah-Peou's life once. What I would give to have saved her life once more! Before she died! You know, Ah-Peou, she would've wanted you guys to do right by those who supported her, who supported you. Remember that. Remember me. I was your babysitter! Those were the best years of my life!"

She burst into tears, streams dripping down her face, clear and glistening, as transparent as the Sprite she'd given Peou in her time of need. "Ah-Peou, how I will miss you!" she cried, grabbing Darren's upper arms, but looking past him, at the giant portrait. Then she stuck her hand in her purse and fished out an eight-ounce water bottle, purple and gold ribbons fastened around it, vertically, over the top and under the bottom—a trick used for extra security on the cheap plastic lids. She pushed the bottle into Darren's hands. "Here, take this! Please, accept my offering, free of charge.

Like you, I am starting to learn business, and my business is selling my secret medicine."

"Bong Vey! There you are." Ming Won approached them from behind, placed her arms on Ohm Vey's shoulders. "Come greet the monks."

"Anything for Peou!" She winked at the three cousins, then left with Ming Won, their arms interlocked.

"What the fuck was that?" Molly said.

"Old Cambo ladies freaking out over this guy's pedigree," Vinny said. "What's new?

"Dude," Darren said, "I can't with this community's obsession with Sprite."

Molly grabbed Darren's arm. "We have shit to debrief."

"I'm supposed to direct people."

"This is an emergency," Molly said, and Vinny nodded.

—

IT WASN'T AN EMERGENCY, AS far as Darren could tell. In the men's bathroom, he leaned his shoulder against the water-stained brown wall, next to a hand dryer that barely worked. He listened intently to Molly and Vinny as they raved about their encounter with the Lort Guy at Mekong Grocery Store. Molly was sitting on the pink granite counter, in between two sinks with gold faucets, while Vinny was two-stepping on the dirty tile, dancing out his nervous energy. Three toilet stalls stood across from the counter, where Molly was idly kicking her feet into the air.

It was insane, they both kept repeating, and Darren hardly understood—not the facts of the story, but why his two cousins were so bent out of shape. Sure, the Lort Guy was sketchy, and mildly despicable in his refusal to become fully independent from his mother. He'd heard from Ming Nary how the Lort Guy and his siblings demanded their mother to cook them different meals each day. They sent their poor mother all over town on the whims of their individual cravings, to buy ingredients from the Cambodian grocery store, the Food 4 Less, the Costco, the farmers' market on the beach, and even the Hispanic and Mediterranean bodegas. You better not end up as entitled and spoiled as that, Ming Nary would tell him.

But Darren wondered: How could the Lort Guy's actions possibly measure up to the other absurd antics they'd witnessed growing up in Cambotown? Was the Lort Guy any more insane, for instance, than Ohm Vey and her pseudoscientific medicinal concoctions? He toyed with the items in his pockets, his phone in his right and the bottle of Sprite in his left, and then lifted himself off the wall. "Okay, but like, the last time I was in Mekong Grocery Store, these two Gongs got in a fistfight."

"Darren." Molly brought her feet onto the counter and placed her forehead onto her knees. "I know you try to always be, like, above everything, but can you, for once, not be so condescending."

"Fuuuuckkkkkkk, shots are being fired," Vinny said, before he let out an OHHHHHH and cupped his mouth, his voice warping into a drone that bounced around the bathroom.

"I don't think I'm above anything. I just think we're gonna waste a ton of brain power if we have a powwow session for every bizarre occurrence we witness. There's no point in trying to extract reasonable explanations from Cambotown. Nothing ever makes sense here. And anyway, I bet the Lort Guy's actions come down to some stupid beef between his family and ours, and that beef, like I've said, probably makes zero sense, probably originated decades ago, probably concerns family members we don't even know, and I bet you anything that it only has to do with us—like the three of us—in the way that our parents try to make everything around here"—he opened his arms wide, making lateral circles in the air—"seem pertinent to our lives, like we have the power to change situations that have nothing to do with us, and thus, by that logic, somehow, everything—and I mean everything!—becomes partly our fault. Fights between our great-great-great ancestors—that's apparently our problem now! That's how shit works, don't you get it? Getting involved is exactly how they trap you in the cage of their screwed-up expectations."

Darren was out of breath, and Vinny only shook his head in response, his feet planted on the ground, as though the time for dancing had arrived and gone. "Nah, bruh," he finally said, "I agree with Molly. Shit is brewing in the air." He pointed an index finger up at the ceiling and made tiny spirals. "And I think it has everything to do with us."

Her forehead still pressed onto her knees, Molly groaned into the crevice between her chest and her thighs and leading to her stomach, the sound a self-imposed gut punch. Then she flung her head back, leaning it against the mirror. Her long hair doubled in the reflection and morphed into a giant black mass—a Rorschach test of Molly's current state. "Can you just be fucking supportive?"

Darren wanted to respond, but only checked his phone. "Fuck, the funeral is about to start."

Suddenly they heard a toilet flush, the struggle of pants being lifted. The door to the middle stall swung open, and the owner of Mekong Grocery hurtled out belly first, his hair greasy and slicked back and approaching a mullet. In the process of tucking his shirt into his pants, his eyes bulging, he grunted as he squeezed his stomach fat to fasten his belt. He was wearing a light gray suit, his jacket hanging over his shoulder, the sight of which made Darren relieved, stupidly so. That someone else in this bathroom was dressed like him, as though this evened the playing field of the cousins' conversation.

Molly jumped off the counter. "I'm sorry, Pou Nhean."

"Oh no, don't mind me," he said. "You kids keep on talking. This is all very interesting." He wiped his hands on his suit pants. "Very, very interesting."

"What's so interesting?" Darren asked.

"Nothing, nothing. I am glad to find out about the commotion in my store this morning." He laughed, holding his belly as it bounced to the bellowing of his voice. "You know, ever since Ah-Peou died, the nom lort has been tasting much better than it ever did. Sugar always tastes better after a death, and your Ming Peou—now that was a big death."

The three cousins exchanged furtive glances.

"Oh, stop being so serious!" he said, laughing again, slipping his arms into the sleeves of his jacket. "Funerals should be a celebration of life. The future! And I, for one, am ready for the future." He flashed a grin and then shuffled out of the bathroom.

"Bruh," Vinny said, "the owner of Mekong Grocery didn't wash his hands."

"You don't need to remind us." Molly said.

"Has Pou Nhean always been so . . . fucking weird?" Darren asked.

"I don't know what's normal and what's not anymore," Molly said, now washing her own hands, as though someone, anyone, had to make up for Pou Nhean's sanitary negligence.

"We should get going," Darren said, only for the bathroom door to fly open, crashing into the wall with a loud thud.

"I've been looking for you guys everywhere!" Ming Won yelled from the hallway. "What're you doing in the men's bathroom? Never mind—just come! Stop dilly-dallying! Come!"

In a sulking daze, the three cousins followed Ming Won out of the bathroom. They braced themselves for the hundreds of relatives to bombard them with performances of grief, with unsolicited advice about the future, the ethics and morals of different Cambotown practices. And upon entering the main room, their nerves were not disappointed. The place was packed with Cambos (and the occasional significant other of a mixed-race couple). The older people in their sixties and beyond were already in their seats, close to the stage, where the monks were sitting cross-legged on the floor, behind a giant spread of food. Kids dressed in white darted through the pews, the crowd, as they ignored their mothers yelling at them to pipe down. A gaggle of solemn Pous stood in the back, most of them in black suits, while a few Mings ran around, handing out water bottles in an illogical, haphazard fashion.

Ming Won slipped her arm through Molly's and led her to a group of Mings and Ohms. "I am tired of answering questions about you, for you," she said, and Molly sighed in defeat.

Are you dating anyone? they asked. *Have you gained weight? Have you lost weight? Tell me pointers, so I can tell my own daughter how to lose weight. What is your career, anyway? Maybe you should start looking for a husband. I have some handsome nephews in Cambodia who very much are dying to obtain green cards. Oh, so you are living at home now. Such a good daughter to realize that there is nothing if not family, nowhere better for a Cambo to live other than in Cambotown. Outside of here, there is nothing for us. Nothing for you. But here, anything is possible.*

That last comment came from Ohm Lee, and Molly wondered, Is this lady's rumored love for that monk so deep, so fulfilling, that she had plunged right into the depths of her longing, into this other way of being and seeing and experiencing? Could even unrequited love create such intense boundaries of where and how potentialities existed? Molly hated the thought of it, how love trapped people in their delusions, and how these delusions often rendered the world false, equipped people with self-serving morals. She wanted to believe in truth, not scientific reason, but emotional clarity, a higher realm of existence. One could be transported to this higher realm by pursuing a stark understanding of reality, which, in her eyes, was best achieved not through love, as evidenced by Ohm Lee's warped stance on Cambotown, but through relentless self-discovery by way of, well, some artistic calling, whether it be an actual art form or a passion developed as though it were one, such as—she hated to admit—Ohm Vey's new medicinal Sprite enterprise. At least Ohm Vey understood what she wanted out of life, which was better than what the hell was going on with Darren.

She wasn't knocking his hustle, but Darren could be a snob, a prick, too quick in using humor as a defense mechanism, and Stanford had fortified these attributes, locked them into place, almost as though her cousin were now stuck on repeat to wax existential. Hopefully, he would come around to their mission. As Ohm Lee lectured her about the nothingness running rampant outside of Cambotown, Molly looked around the room for more signs of disturbances of their natural order, as though she could drive some tangible proof out of the shadows for Darren to witness. Maybe the Lort Guy or the Lort Guy's mother or any of the Lort Guy's siblings—or perhaps a man in a Dodgers cap—would be in attendance at the funeral?

But there were too many people crowding the room. She could hardly parse out who from who, and she needed to prepare herself mentally for her eulogy, anyway. She caught Vinny's glance, who was standing with his two henchmen and Darren. Her brother gave her a nod, a smirk, a reassurance that he'd lure their cousin over to their side—wherever that was. She nodded in response. Then she answered the questions of her mother's friends.

Across the room, Vinny was listening to Kelvin and Rithy debate the pros and cons of the Khmai Kong Rappers finding a temporary summer sublet in Cambotown. They delivered their points in a stilted manner. Both had already resigned themselves to the idea of living with their respective parents, to save money before their tour, but neither possessed the emotional bandwidth to engage in small talk about grief, the deceased, or even the concept of death itself.

"Death is wild," Rithy had said earlier, but Vinny ignored him. He was too busy thinking about his morning scuffle with the Lort Guy. It had been invigorating to chase after that sketchy motherfucker, had induced Vinny with the same thrills as rapping onstage. But now he was concerned that Darren would be missing all the fun, that his cousin's critical self-loathing would ruin this chance for much-needed familial bonding, and worse yet, that this unfolding mystery had everything to do with Peou's Cambotown reputation, and that him, his baby sis, and his dear cousin had been charged by Peou's ghost to steer her legacy into its appropriate place in history. If Darren didn't soon jump on board to their mission command, the whole ship would crash and sink to be forever lost in the annals of Cambotown history.

Of course, in writing this, I might be overdetermining Vinny's motivations. Concerning the funeral, Vinny, in our conversations, had the haziest memory of our three protagonists. (Molly would later intimate to me that Vinny was lacking in a historical self, that he only ever inhabited his self-self. Her actual words for her brother were more along the lines of "self-centered" and "excessive egomaniac," but in my margin notes, I wrote "sibling bias?" for a reason I don't exactly remember.) Let's just say this: at that moment, Vinny was sincerely concerned about Darren's response in the bathroom, his cousin's hesitancy just another sign of a growing distance, another hitch in his plans for the official tour of the Khmai Kong Rappers—a bad omen.

Now Rithy was saying, "Fuck, man, I'm gonna miss our Oakland pad."

"Wait," Darren said. "You guys are moving out of Oakland?"

"We've been talking about it for the past ten minutes," Kelvin said.

"You didn't tell me that," Darren said, turning toward his cousin.

"Sometimes you listen with your ears but not much else," Vinny said.

"I'm just . . . surprised. You guys moved there super recently."

"Yeah, and our business in Oakland is now done. We finished recording our album."

"But you have an apartment."

"Oh, none of that shit was mine. I live with a light step."

"I was under the impression we were gonna drive back to the Bay."

"Things have come up, and there's business, like, right here, that I—we—gotta tend to, remember?"

Darren clutched the phone and bottle in their respective pockets, grabbed onto what he could as he felt the vertigo of time slipping from under his feet. "You're really, just, making moves with your life, then."

"Yeah, I am."

For a few moments, nobody said anything. The cousins avoided eye contact. Their two friends shifted in place, suspended in the tension between the cousins.

"Darren," Rithy finally said, "we've been meaning to ask you. What the hell are you studying in your schooling?"

"We've been hearing about you studying, like, business or some shit," Kelvin said, tossing his head back to indicate his sources as the gaggle of Pous.

Their words cut through the silence like a butter knife would a pig carcass. Devoid of slick elegance, jagged and awkward, tone-deaf but safe in their utter ineffectiveness, Kelvin and Rithy had the elocutionary grace of clueless adolescents.

"Yeah," Rithy said, "none of us know shit about what you do at Stanford. But I know you aren't some MBA-minded fool. You aren't Kenny with his boba Ziplocs. And you're light-years away from the fools in my online accounting classes at Comm."

"Oh well," Darren said, "it depends on if I get this scholarship I applied for. If I win it, my funding would increase, and I'd have a stronger network and clout, which might guarantee me a tenure-track job as a professor, though I'm not really committed to a life as a teacher, and I'm not even sure if universities will, like, even survive or be standing in fifty years. Mostly I want my current paycheck to double. Palo Alto's expensive as fuck. Anyway, the scholarship would lock me into my dissertation topic—you know, like the research and book I have to write for my PhD—because my work would have to fit into the values of the foundation, and align with what I proposed in my application, in which I said I'd be writing about the philosophical origins of comedy and its epistemological relation to trauma theory, how both revel in the fragmentary, broken nature of reality."

Rithy and Kelvin looked at him blankly.

"Glad to know you're doing the good work," Vinny said with solemn sarcasm.

"I mean," Darren said, "I kind of hate the idea of writing a book on humor and trauma. It feels trite. Like, for example, Cambos here are always laughing, but it's not only because they are trying to heal from their pain. Sometimes old Cambo dudes laugh because they are just, you know, laughing."

"What do you want to write about, then?" Kelvin asked, as he texted on his phone.

"I'm not sure. I'm just following the money."

"You're saying you're tryna sell out," Vinny said, and before Darren could respond, before he could even begin to formulate a defense, a comeback, the coterie of monks on the stage issued an ethereal droning, with the head monk muttering Khmer chants into a mic. Several Mas in the back row repeated the chants in a robotic unison, establishing a call-and-response, a signal to shut the fuck up, and everyone dropped their conversations and headed to their seats.

When the rows filled up, the younger generation, from teenagers to toddlers, spilled onto the floor, tucked their ankles under their asses, bowed their heads down like they'd been taught to do at the temple. Lining the perimeter of the room, leaning against the walls, were Pous with bad knees and too-cool-for-school Cambo prohs, including Kelvin and Rithy, their hands pressed together and fingertips against their foreheads.

Darren and Vinny found their mothers and Molly sitting on the ground, right by the stage, right under Peou's closed casket. As the chanting continued, Molly wished she could deliver her eulogy to Peou's face. Maybe if she could see her face, something would click, a vision of truth would appear, but Molly knew that was impossible. Peou's scorched body was hardly recognizable after the car crash. Nothing would be more traumatic than opening that casket for the duration of the funeral and letting a corpse supersede everyone's memory of her Ming.

Kneeling to Molly's left, his chest pressed against his folded knees, his forehead balancing on the ground, Vinny looked as though he were sleeping. Ming Won reached in front of Darren to push her son awake, only to realize he was chanting along to the monks. Her son was entranced. He had fallen into a reverie. Vinny was the only cousin—hell, the sole Cambo his age—who remembered the Buddhist recitations, and though he barely understood the monks' low hum of Khmer, he could still imitate their intonations. He felt perfectly at ease in that ancient cadence, and basking in those celestial rhythms, breathing and praying in the space between life and death, Vinny found the melody of this song dedicated to Peou's life. Vinny swore he could feel Peou's spirit dimming in and out of its current limbo state. She was giving into the wave of their crooning. She needed those in attendance of the funeral to carry her forth into a new reincarnated life. He thought he was doing all he could to alleviate that final heartbreaking transition. *Don't worry about us*, he wanted to sing to the beat, *start fresh, start anew, we will dance in your remembrance.*

In a compromised prayer stance, sitting to Vinny's left, Darren was crying. Was that what his mother had in mind when telling him to represent as the man of the family?

That he would be sobbing in his suit, dripping onto his shirt. Kneeling in his slacks, it was impossible to bend his legs beneath his weight, comfortably, properly, and then to crouch forward into a bow. Unlike Molly and Vinny and Ming Won and Ming Nary, who were almost completely horizontal, their bodies contorted and stacked into three layers, torso in line with thighs in line with calves, Darren tried balancing himself upright, without holding on to the ground, as his hands needed to be clasped together, but his upper body kept slipping over his folded legs, even with his shoes off. And so he kept fidgeting, breaking in and out of praying, to catch himself from falling. He was placed in the middle of his family, Vinny and Molly to his right, Ming Won and Ming Nary to his left. He was the closest person to the monks who were facing them directly. He felt exposed by the glare of those orange robes, a blinding light intoning indistinguishable words, a holy tableau of monks and food and Peou in her deathbed, all passing judgment onto him—this sobbing man-child who couldn't embody the grace, the serenity, the deep calm of a masculine grief, to sit still even for twenty minutes of praying. Darren wanted to be humble, to invoke within himself that stoic manner a family needs in their eldest son, but he could not stop fidgeting, and he could not lower his head to the ground. He sat upright, tall, subject to all the pressures and judgment surrounding him. He felt both weighed down and unable to topple completely to the floor.

The monks stopped chanting. People on the ground lifted their torsos from their knees. Those sitting in the pews raised their foreheads from their clasped hands. As Molly stood up to deliver her eulogy, Darren pulled out his phone and checked his email. He needed to distract himself, to turn away from those monks, to hide his tears from everyone else, because they belonged to him and no one else, not the monks, not even his mother. The email app started refreshing, and suddenly it all overwhelmed him, the idea of listening to his cousin talk about his dead Ming in front of so many Cambos. Why should he and his two cousins share their expressions of grief with anyone but each other?

Right as Molly walked onto the stage, he saw the email. He skimmed "your work deeply impressed us" before "an unprecedented amount of applications" before "unfortunately" before "the waitlist" before "position by mid-September" before he was crawling away from his seat on the ground.

"Bruh, you're gonna miss the main event," Vinny said, and Darren ignored both him and his mother, who tried to push him back into his spot when he passed her by.

"Where do you think you're going?" Ming Nary whispered. "Just hold it in if you need to go to the bathroom." But the burning incense was more pungent than ever. The edges of the room had extended into an infinite blur of bodies and faces taunting him, faces from his childhood he had thought, fearfully and hopefully, he would resemble, faces who had been watching him his entire life, faces he now realized had always skulked in his peripheral vision, ready to attack, to recruit, to indoctrinate, with their pursed lips and expectant eyes, which were cruel in their glimmers of misguided sympathy and smothering empathy. The suspicions he'd been carrying since his youth were clarifying in his mind as he stumbled his way to the side door, shuffling on his hands and knees, trying his best to avoid eye contact, to remove himself from the crowd's line of vision. As he approached the door, Darren looked back, and Molly saw the tears in his eyes, the heaving of his chest, as she walked up to the podium. She grimaced at her cousin's emotional display. She nodded, urging Darren out of the audience.

Baked into her words, even if she wasn't entirely conscious of it, Molly's eulogy carried a purpose beyond the honoring of her Ming's spirit. Her eulogy had no business with Darren.

—

OUTSIDE IN THE FOYER, DARREN stared at Peou's canvas portrait, gazed into her pixelated eyes. When the throbbing in his chest lessened and his breathing relaxed, he looked up at the triptych of paintings. He focused on the band of men in the Bruegel reproduction. Maybe it did make sense that they could see a forward path only in the open sea. The half-built tower appeared to Darren as a massive burden. If it had been completely destroyed, then the landscape, the village, the community, might have been salvageable. Instead, this useless, immovable obstruction was lodged into the very earth.

Finally, Darren broke free from the cheap reproduction, from the spell of his own gaze. He turned toward the main room, where Pou Sith was pacing in front of the doors, his shoulders hunched over, strides jerky, violent, twitching in a robotic spasm. As Darren approached him, Pou Sith began to shake his head and curse under his breath.

"Pou, what's wrong?"

"What is wrong with you stupid kids! Go ahead, tell me!"

"Wait, what're you talking about?"

"I will not take this disrespect anymore. You better support your two cousins now, because they are trash to me! You think I won't disown them?" He pointed directly at Darren's chest. "Hah! You must be kidding yourself. I raised and supported those two trash children of mine their entire lives, and now my daughter has humiliated me in front of everyone I know! I am done. It is over. I have no kids. You be their parent. See how much respect you get, how crazy they drive you!"

Pou Sith stormed away and exited the building to the front parking lot. Darren watched his backside get smaller and smaller. He wondered if Pou Sith was going to "man up this time" (as Molly had also wondered aloud about her father) and actually do it—leave forever, that is—if he'd drive off into the Southern Californian horizon, like Darren's own father, or if this was just another classic tantrum so recognizable among that older generation of immature men. Was life just watching those closest to you exhibit the same patterns of behavior through the unfurling decades?

Curious to know what had jolted Pou Sith into this angry frenzy, Darren entered the main room, right as Molly spoke the last words of her eulogy. He looked into the crowd. He saw the rippling of a communal anger, muted expressions of discomfort, the contoured wrinkles and gaping mouths that embellish the offended.

Sometimes Darren swore he could see the very creation of shared feelings, the binding of people into a culture, or a subculture, or even just a petty social clique. Usually, it was triggered by a transgression of the status quo. A member of a community upsets another, whether publicly or privately (only to be made public later), and while you can hope that people will, more or less, split evenly into the different camps of the offended and the offender, that both sides are legitimate in their own right and obtain their just amount of backing, that an inherent sense of democracy is upheld, that the problems of life can be solved through a suitably porous, evolving two-party system, what mostly happens, especially in established group dynamics, is that the long-standing belief snuffs out the transgression. People look to past behavior and attitudes as truths in themselves. The creation of a shared feeling so often becomes the recirculation of old beliefs, a doubling down fueled by mass hysteria, a gang mentality squashing the sparks of revolution.

But if you can make your transgression potent enough, logical enough, and then heard and digested, acknowledged and reckoned with, you can cut straight through a group of people. You can reconfigure new affinities. That was the magic of comedy, the philosophical core. That was what Plato didn't understand. Yes, it could be true, Plato's superiority theory of humor. Comedy has a propensity for determining some people superior over others. Witnesses of a joke are often laughing at the expense of an unfortunate fool who slips or self-harms. But of course Plato, being the arrogant fool he was, shirked the idea of a punch line subverting the established order of authority, the hierarchy and scaffolding of society, so that even a great Stoic could lose his hold over his pupils, becoming the butt of a joke at the will of a smart enough, skilled enough, class clown. And aren't some types of people, depending on the contexts of your unfortunate history, officially deemed to be clowns, lesser than beings, minorities? And wouldn't this mean that humor was one of a few ways in which these clowns could finally claim their rightful superiority? Darren knew this well, how you could deliver a joke so gut-punching, with such precise timing, that the audience's varying visceral responses would forge new alliances and expose fossilized connections. Two persons on different sides laugh at the same joke. Two persons on different sides are rendered complicit with some taboo offensive subject. Two persons previously in cahoots are now dragged apart, their differing responses to the joke at hand prying open a crack in their bond, a disagreement they've ignored until now. In the best-case scenario, everyone's laughing too hard to care, really, that their world has been shaken into a new configuration, and this new configuration, ideally, pushes everyone to reexamine their previous biases, which were probably outdated, and even harmful, anyway.

If only life worked the way comedy, or art, or music, did. Where you can manipulate these momentous transgressions for the greater good. If only Darren didn't look into the audience of the funeral, and then at Molly on the stage, and witness the affirmation of some preconceived notion that was now gearing up against his cousin and, thus, against all three of them. But there was no longer time for Darren's convoluted thoughts.

—

THE MONKS STOOD UP AND started chanting again. Molly moved to the edge of the stage. Right below her, Ming Won and Ming Nary directed people to their next locations, their hand motions an aggressive, artful orchestration. Darren rushed to the stage, where he joined Vinny, Kelvin, Rithy, and five other young Cambo prohs and Pous in carrying Peou's casket, from the stage to the door, down the hallway and leading to the backyard. The men followed Molly, Ming Won, and Ming Nary, who were following the chanting monks, who were following Mr. Abelman. Another twenty or so Cambos, the ones who had felt closest to Peou (or who were the most compelled to prove their loyalty), such as Ohm Vey and Ohm Lee, were a few steps behind, while the majority of the funeral attendees were left in the main room.

The cousins knew what would happen next. This, no one was hiding from them. This part was as clear as day. They were prepared, had expected to undergo this upcoming formality since they were teenagers, though they hadn't known it would be for Peou. It was a ritual that somehow was developed in Cambotown. Maybe it was a long-standing tradition from back in the golden age of Cambodia. Darren, Molly, and Vinny didn't know. They had never asked. And, really, who'd even verify the answers they'd receive?

Everyone crammed into the detached building. A daunting furnace spanned the entire westward wall, taking up a third of the floor space. The men placed the casket on a metal table, with its edge, where Peou's feet lay, at the furnace's gaping mouth. The monks lined up behind the casket, almost pressed against the wall. Darren, Molly, and Vinny were pushed by their mothers to the front of the crowd, right across from the monks, who had started chanting louder than before, despite now being in a smaller room, their faces scrunched into an aggressive concentration.

The crowd kneeled onto the ground and resumed praying. Ming Won and Ming Nary lit sticks of incense and passed them around for everyone to hold in their hands. Mr. Abelman squeezed into a dark corner of the room, by the side of the furnace, and swiveled several knobs in a precise fashion, which ignited a flame inside the machine that now roared awake, yawning out a gasoline blast of hot air. The sound crashed into the monk's chanting, and Darren, Molly, and Vinny leaned into one another, propping themselves up into a united force, as they prayed in the center of this spiritual torrent of clashing energies. The cousins grounded themselves to withstand the battering of the monks' chanting. The heat of the furnace burned the left sides of their faces. The monks raised their clasped hands up and over their heads, before swinging their arms back down, over and over again, as though beating Peou's spirit to stay in its wooden prison, to not fight its entrance into that fiery portal. From behind, the cousins felt the crowd's presence brushing against their backs, pushing them forward, but they stayed in place, praying, crying, focused on keeping each other firmly planted.

They were all weeping. Some older Mas wailed at the top of their lungs. The rhythm of the monks chanting had been overtaken by the primal force of communal grief. Every new death these Mas witnessed unlocked the memories of every old death they had mourned. So tragic it was to endure the deaths of both those older and younger than you! Darren, Vinny, and Molly felt their limbs turn to jelly. The layers of their consciousness, their defensive walls, their reactionary emotions, peeled away so that they were raw, tender flesh.

Ming Nary crawled her way through the crowd, then tapped the cousins to stand up. She pointed for them to stand at the end of Peou's casket. Ming Won had taken Mr. Abelman's place at the control panel. She pushed a button, kept her hand pressed on it as her tears tapped into a deeper well for crying, as the mouth of the furnace opened, a blazing gust blasting into the room. The head monk was sprinkling holy water onto the casket. The other monks raised their clasped hands up and down more vigorously. Still holding their sticks of incense, the cousins started pushing the casket. They pushed and pushed against the pressure of that burning air, their feet gripping the tile floor. They swore their hands could feel Peou's dead skull through the wood. The casket slowly slid into the furnace, then landed into the flames with an explosive thud. Ming Won let go of the button, and the closing mechanical mouth produced an ear-popping rusty screech. Then there was the silence of Peou's body in flames, of tears dripping down faces. The monks had finally stopped chanting. Everyone looked exhausted. They were defeated. It was yet another death, but the adults in the room knew that this one would be cataclysmic. The cousins knew, too, but only through the narrow scope of their own perspective. The cousins had no sense of the peripheral consequences as Peou's spirit was being released into the atmosphere, in gentle waves of warmth that emanated from the furnace, that lapped their skin in heady shocks.

With no one uttering a word, the crowd shuffled out

of the detached building. Most of the party set off for the main room, where they would watch the monks eat their food, waiting patiently before grabbing their own individual plates. Darren, Molly, and Vinny stood outside by the detached building. Their mothers signaled for them to follow, but they needed some fresh air.

"I'm sorry for missing your eulogy," Darren said.

"You didn't need to hear it," Molly said.

"She rocked the room, my baby sis," Vinny said, wrapping his arm around Molly's head and messing up her hair. "Ming Peou would've been proud."

Molly pushed her brother off. "I feel sick."

"I have something for that," Darren said. He pulled Ohm Vey's product out of his pocket and tossed it to Molly.

After shooting Darren a skeptical look, Molly rotated the bottle in her hand, examined how it splintered sunlight into faint gold streaks. She twisted off the cap and gulped down a third of the concoction, that mix of American invention, industrial chemicals, with roots pulled from Ohm Vey's backyard, before she passed the bottle to Vinny, who did the same and returned it to Darren. Then Darren finished the bottle off. The fumes of the incense and the ashes of their Ming collected over them. The drink fizzed in their stomachs. They stalled for that crashing wave of numbness, half-expecting, despite those influences whirling above and around, for nothing to happen.

DINNER WITH THE CORE FAMILY

FICTION, FROM *STRAIGHT THRU CAMBOTOWN*

Their first meal together after the funeral, a rejuvenation, a cleanse, or that was how Ming Nary pitched it. "Eat this, oun, what're you waiting for? Eat!" Ming Nary said in one breath, shoving plates of sliced beef, the strips glistening raw pink, into the hands of Darren and then Molly and Vinny. "You need to flush the toxins of American food out of your system," Ming Nary continued, now talk-shouting, now almost throwing pea shoots and even rawer beef slices at the fully grown kids of her family. "I know you eat trash box food. I should have never bought you that microwave. You know how many hormones American companies inject into our food? Chickens shouldn't be that fat. It's disturbing. We're being poisoned living over here. Every day, we eat poison. Every. Single. Day—poison."

In the center of the dining table, a pot of boiling broth sat on a lit burner, emitted burning steam, a fish sauce stench, into the already hot air of Battambang Bai. Karaoke videos looped on three flat-screen televisions fastened to the walls, all featuring the same floppy-haired man wearing too much foundation, a shade too light for his skin. A week had passed since they witnessed Peou's holy incineration.

Encircling the table counter clockwise, they were seated in the following order: Pou Sith with arms crossed over pudgy stomach fat, every finger laced in gold rings, rolled into fists and ready to punch out any potential threat, flimsy sunglasses still on as though he needed a screen of protection between him and his own family, as though his two idiot children were said potential threat, especially Molly, his daughter always the one digging her ungrateful attitude into the tender, bruised flesh of his ego; then Ming Won, deep bags under her eyes, with hair pulled tightly into a bun because she could hardly tolerate even the minuscule nonsense of her own loose strands of hair, Ming Won who was angry herself at Molly, but mostly annoyed at her husband for incessantly talking about his own childish anger at their children, disrupting her work in calling, and personally thanking, every Cambo over forty who had attended the funeral; then Vinny, already high from a morning joint for this family brunch, in an oversized black Gucci T-shirt, forehead wrapped in a yellow folded bandanna, his feet tapping to the beat of the new song that had been formulating in his mind all week, an elegy for Peou, because he was actually pumped by Molly's eulogy, had thought it was totally hilarious, had wanted to cheer and holler in response while listening in the audience of the funeral, and now, he had determined, it was his turn to honor their Ming, the torch having been passed from his baby sis to him; then Molly, now having resorted to wearing her mother's stiff work clothes, bought from the double-clearance section of Nordstrom Rack, until she could replace her lost hipster wardrobe of high-waisted light denim jeans and cheap-looking expensive crop tops, with her paranoias, her grudge against the Lort Guy, sitting on the back burner of her mind and her anxiety about money and finding a job claiming its rightful place at the forefront, which also meant that she was, for the most part, unaware that her parents remained furious at her, because weren't they always fuming over something, anyway?; then Darren, his goatee long, unkempt, and frizzing out so that everyone hated it, except Vinny, who'd kept calling him "our resident philosopher," Darren the "cranky wiseguy oracle motherfucker," Darren who was exhausted from helping his mother all week, as whenever he visited home, she refused to drive, claimed her osteoporosis made it impossible for her to step on the pedals of her car, so he always became her personal chauffeur, dropping her off and picking her up from the DMV, accompanying her all over Cambotown on her epic quests for the most organic and healthy of produce, as if antioxidants were enough to dispel the trauma running through her and her only son's blood, though Darren, for this visit at least, secretly reveled in the excuse to distract himself with his mother's peculiarities, as his scholarship wait-list had totally extinguished his motivation to work on his dissertation proposal, now due in less than two months, now almost impossible for him to conceive of finishing, given the prospect that he might be getting paid less than he would have wanted, to think he'd waste the rest of his twenties actually doing the hard work of a PhD student; then Ming Nary, trying to support Ming Won and Pou Sith's rage against her kmouy srei, as she had only one sister left, so she should always be supporting her last surviving sibling, right, but all week she had been torn when listening to her sister complain about her brother-in-law complain about her kmouy srei, to the point that her insurmountable anxiety required her to go into full detox mode with her diet, because at the end of the day, she thought Molly had gotten Peou right in her eulogy, had captured the way Peou thought and felt and moved through the world, and who cares if what Molly said might have been offensive? What would it matter? How bad could it be for the men in Cambotown to get called out once in a while? Oh, how she wished that she (or anyone, really) had cursed out her ex-husband when he abandoned her and their only child!

Finally, between Ming Nary and Pou Sith there was an empty chair. The three cousins were oblivious, stuck in their own winding thoughts, when Ming Won had stopped the waitress from clearing away the extra place setting. The waitress was named Soramee, and she had also happened to hear about Molly's eulogy, from her own Ming, known as Ohm Lee to everyone else, whom she drove three times a week to the temple. During each of these drives, she listened to Ohm Lee monologue about true love, how only devout, loyal, and adamant women discover and obtain it, and, of course, that was how the topic of Molly came up—Molly, that terror of a daughter, what Ohm Lee once described to Ming Won as "having been born in the wrong womb," that old Khmer idiom reserved for those daughters, like Molly, who just couldn't shut up, who couldn't accept their mothers as the definitive guiding source of their lives, who definitely would be cursed with a lifetime of loneliness, with their foolish whims and ideas about what was and was not wrong. But Soramee mentioned none of this as she served the family. She brought plate after plate of raw beef and pork, shrimps with their beady heads intact, greasy fish and pork balls, slabs of silken tofu and slices of jellyfish, spinach and bon chok and other leafy greens with no English names, enoki and shiitake and oyster mushrooms, and fresh egg noodles paired with steaming bowls of white rice. And she definitely shut her mouth when, out of nowhere, as he fished for a cooked plump shrimp in the communal pot, twirling through the broth with his chopsticks, Darren said:

"I'm gonna buy a bus ticket back to the Bay Area tonight."

His mother dropped her soup spoon into her bowl. The scalding broth splashed onto her hand. "What?—why?" she said, wincing in pain, sucking on her burned hand. "I thought you were on summer vacation!"

"How many times do I need to tell you?" Darren said. "Grad school isn't like regular school. Just because I have no classes, doesn't mean I don't have work. Actually, classes are the least stressful part."

"Don't be fooled by his hoopla," Vinny said, grinning and looking around at everyone. "He doesn't need to be anywhere his family isn't at."

"What're you talking about?" Ming Won said, slapping Vinny on the head. "He needs to finish school."

"Just let him go," Molly said, and it was up in the air, even to herself, whether she was defending Darren or just tired of him, his bullshit, his condescending reluctance.

"Okay, but I don't need to finish grad school," Darren said. "It's not like I can't survive without this PhD. It's not like getting a bachelor's." He regretted that last part because Ming Won, for years, had been railing on Vinny's lack of a college degree, unrelenting in her comments that her son could still enroll in community college classes, then transfer to a UC, then get an actual decent job, then attract a respectable woman to marry, all before the age of forty, when unmarried men become lost into a "forever childhood."

"You speak nonsense!" Ming Nary said. "You tell me that you have to leave home—leave me!—for school, even though you have no class, but that you also don't need this degree, that it's not important. So, what is it, then? How are we supposed to understand you when you don't give us a clear understanding!"

Darren was about to respond when Ming Won stood up, with a sudden air of formality, her chair sliding back on the hardwood with a scratchy resonance. "Come, come," she yelled, waving her hand back toward herself. She walked around Pou Sith and pulled out the empty chair. Ming Nary wiped the broth from her mouth, then also stood up, aligning her body with her sister's. Vinny was busy revising the chorus of his new song—"Circling the block with her refugee money, don't fuck with her brown skin she always surviving, even now that she gone all over still are the bodies she been burying"—so, only Darren and Molly looked over to where their mothers' attention was directed. Only they felt the shock, the initial sickening dread, the cathartic boom and sinking of rightful paranoia, as they beheld the sight, the vision, of the man with a Dodgers cap stepping out of their haunted minds and now approaching their table.

Molly clutched Darren's shirtsleeve. The man took steady,

careful steps, and his eyes were huge and bulging, Molly thought, almost like a frog's. When she was a child, she thought the same thing of the yellowing black-and-white photo of her father's father, the old teacher, who was also equipped with protruding amphibian eyeballs that seemed to be staring at her always, wherever she was, even when she was nowhere near their dining room, his expression piercing and judgmental and overbearing, a masculine presence haunting her through life. She wasn't religious, could care less about the validity of the monks, the afterlife, or reincarnation, but how could you not believe in angry ghosts, a cosmic imbalance of the world, when for your entire life you stared at creepy-ass photos of your family members killed in a genocide? When the man you thought was following your every move, just a week prior, was hugging your mother and Ming, when he was sitting down at your family's brunch table, ordering a Vietnamese coffee from the waitress, whom you've seen working at this same restaurant for over a decade?

"Hello, everyone," the man said, neatly folding a napkin over his thighs. He was wearing a brown leather jacket over a T-shirt stained with oil and drenched in sweat, what the cousins would later learn was his standard outfit, his choice uniform in performing his duties, along with that Dodgers cap he never took off.

Everyone made a gesture of acknowledgment, from Pou Sith's shrug to Darren's raised eyebrows to Molly's rapid blinking to Vinny saying, "Wassup, man, how are you surviving this hot-ass day with that nice, vintage-ass jacket?"

In her seat again, Ming Won slapped Vinny once more. "This is Pou—"

"Please, please," the man said, "just call me Anchaly and also, Vinny"—he tilted his head down—"I like to feel like I am back in the Cambodian humidity. Sweating is good for you, releases all the bad stuff."

"See," Ming Nary said, "this is why we are eating hot pot!"

"That's a cool trick," Vinny said, his elbows on the table, face cupped in his hands. "Dropping my name like that."

"So, who are you?" Molly asked.

"He worked with your Ming Peou," Ming Won said.

Molly almost fell back in her chair. Bemused, Vinny cocked his head. Something in Darren—he felt it most in his chest but also through his whole body, and even his thoughts were percolating—finally clicked, and he said, "You're here to disclose information about Ming Peou, about her death, aren't you—Anchaly?"

Anchaly crossed both his arms and legs and grinned, not mischievously but with a cocky grace, as though he were the kind of man that could handle any problem thrown at him, with his brown leather jacket over that shirt he hardly cared about, that shirt that could always take yet another beating. The cousins noticed his missing teeth, one from the upper-right row, and the other the lower left, and they had the thought that occurred to every Cambo kid of their generation when they contemplated the adults of their lives: Was that damage done before, during, or after the genocide?

"You can say that," Anchaly said.

"How are your kids?" Ming Nary asked, ignoring the cousins' jaw-dropped rigidity.

"Oh, who knows, really!" he said. "They are busy with their studies. They text me, 'Dad, can't answer the phone I am in the library,' like they think I am a fool, that I don't keep track of how many times they tell me they are studying in the library. If it was all truth, then why aren't they freaking valedictorians, or getting scholarships, you know?"

"Your wife was too easy on them when they were kids," Ming Won said, with a familiarity that rankled Molly.

"This is why you're here?" Molly said. "To complain about your kids in college?"

Anchaly uncrossed his legs, leaned forward, and placed his elbows on the table. His interwoven hands formed a pedestal for his chin to rest on. His eyes were looking up as though he were strategizing his next step with someone directly above him, or maybe his own brain. "No, you are right," he said. "We should get to business."

The cousins waited for him to say something next, but Anchaly didn't say anything. Each person just stared at the opposite party in a brutal, farcical silence. Each cousin expected one of the adults to play the next move, because weren't the legit adults in their lives always forcing their hands, their wills, toward whatever they wanted, regardless? Each cousin refused to take the first step into this new chapter of their brunch conversation, this new relationship with Anchaly, with Peou, in case that step into the beyond rendered one vulnerable to an unforeseen ambush. Molly wanted only answers. She wanted Anchaly to say something that would provide clarity on any quandary of her life in which she required direction—sure, there was the thrill of receiving information that would stir the evolving conspiracy with the Lort Guy into more action, but she was not so immature, so reckless, to ignore that her life would much appreciate any available financial, professional, emotional, romantic, or quasi-spiritual guidance.

Darren, for his part, hoped that whatever Peou (by way of Anchaly) had to say would not take up too much time, that it would be a closed loop, a direct route between what needed to be said and what needed to be done, with a final and foreseeable blessing of closure. Lately, every new day was yet more evidence that life could be defined as the slow unraveling of more chaos, an entropic motion from the contained bliss of being in your mother's womb to the graphic eviction of birth to the inexorable disorder of daily existence that only knew growth and consumption. As in: if you weren't careful, the chaos would eat you alive. And unlike Molly, who looked straight into this surging volatility, thinking, Maybe there's a hidden logic, maybe we could salvage and heal ourselves, Darren felt that the best-case scenario was to retreat into yourself, and flee once the opportunity was presented. Life was about minimizing the inevitable damage to the psyche, the soul—the constant pain, guilt, and uncertainty that must surely be afflicting every Cambo, whether they believed it or not.

But Vinny knew what would happen the best. He saw in Anchaly a familiarity that had been present their entire lives, in the background of their schooling and upbringing, because Vinny had spent two decades noticing Anchaly's same smirk on Ming Peou's face, how it warped her expression to highlight that inclination of daring, that hunger for self-actualization. Wasn't this what their Ming had preached in the way she moved through Cambotown, to strive forth, always, into the finest version of one's life?

That way of being was what they had cemented into their manifesto, which he still repped, hard, at least. Here, sitting at their table, with that supreme smirk every Cambo kid should be idealizing, across from the boiling meat that only Pou Sith was now eating, was the carrier of a new test, sent from the afterlife, of what really mattered in the cousins' souls. Vinny predicted that in the near future, the next few weeks, his destiny would be bound, tighter than ever before, to the destinies of his dear cousin and baby sis. If they passed this upcoming test, it'd be everyone smiling and laughing. It'd be a celebration, an affirmation, of their brilliance. Vinny had always been one to honor complexity and ignore complications.

Soramee, the waitress, cleared the plates Pou Sith had just emptied. She relit the hot pot's burner. In the silence, they heard the flame spurred by the gasoline and the broth sizzling and Pou Sith chewing and swallowing his last bite, before he whisked off his sunglasses.

"Oh come on already!" he groaned. "I know what you're going to say—Peou left these ungrateful kids her money! These kids, who've never worked a day in their lives, they get to reap the riches of this whole goddamn place."

Anchaly laughed. "As usual, Bong, you are right and wrong at the same time."

"Just tell us already!" Molly said.

"Peou left all her money to her kmouys," Anchaly said, waving his hand at the cousins.

Pou Sith scoffed and threw his used napkin onto his plate.

"Awwwww shiitttttttt," Vinny said, "we're fucking rich."

"Are you serious?" Molly said, exhaling the words right out of Darren's mouth.

Nervous glances ping-ponged around the table. Ming Won and Ming Nary looked as shocked as the cousins. They had no idea if their children could handle this money responsibly, and even though neither, right then, wanted to be hurt, they were. Their little sister had shortchanged them.

"Do you have the will?" Ming Won asked.

"Of course," Anchaly said, "of course."

"How much money is it?" Darren asked.

Anchaly leaned back into his chair, placed his hands on his head, and sighed into a stretch of his spine. He stared up at the ceiling. "That I do not know."

Ming Nary gasped, and Ming Won rolled her eyes, grunting and crossing her arms.

Jarred by their reactions, Molly looked from her mother to her Ming, then back to her mother, then at Anchaly's chin pointed at her, then, again, her eyes rested on her mother. "What the fuck does that mean?" she said to Anchaly, still facing Ming Won.

"Language," Ming Nary said.

"Have respect," Ming Won said.

"It's because of the Circle of Money stuff, isn't it?" Darren said.

"Why is this a guessing game!" Molly cried. "You obviously know what's going on, so just tell us already!"

Anchaly's head snapped forward, and he raised his hands as though caught red-handed. "The money needs to be collected. Whatever amount that needs to be collected"—he lowered his arms and wheeled his right hand into a tiny tornado, shaking his head—"I do not know, but I do know it needs to be collected. Ad then, once it's collected, it also needs to be redistributed back to everyone who is owed money—I mean, whatever amount each person is owed, which I will not know until we know how much money there is to collect—and then, finally, you will get the money Peou has designated to you."

Ming Won's head fell. She shielded her eyes with her hand. Ming Nary's hand flew to cover her mouth, suppressing another gasp, stuffing it back down her throat. Vinny drummed his head to an arrhythmic beat. Darren stretched out his locked jaw, wider and wider, until he reached a painful crack. Molly violently tousled her hair into a mess, a tangled curtain falling over her face, and then gave a yelp into the dark shroud.

"Woah, baby sis," Vinny said, "you still do that?"

"How do we get this money?" Molly said, flipping her hair from her vision but not fixing it.

"You go and collect," Ming Won said, cutting off Anchaly, who held his breath, and then said:

"Yes, what your mother said, but the collections this time around"—he paused, looked at his phone—"it's a strange cycle. I'm not sure what to make of it."

"Hold up," Vinny said, and here, at this point in the conversation, you might ask yourself, Why would Peou go off her routine course? I'm sure, somewhere deep in the cousins' minds, they wondered this, but don't fault them for being so overwhelmed by the present moment, the immediate aftermath of witnessing their Ming incinerated into another cosmic realm, to the point that they weren't asking Anchaly the obvious questions. "What the hell is your job, anyway?"

Anchaly stood up, ignoring the question. He pushed his chair under the table.

"You can't just go," Darren said. "You dropped this bomb on us, and now you're not gonna explain it—anymore than that. Where the hell should we even start collecting?"

"There's nothing more to explain, not yet," Anchaly said. "You will hear from me again, soon."

Ming Nary whacked Darren's arm. "See, now you can't go! You have to wait for Anchaly!"

"I heard," Darren said, and then left the table and headed for the bathroom, in the opposite direction of Anchaly.

In Darren and Anchaly's absence, no one said a word. Soon Pou Sith was stuffing his face again, piling food onto his plate, drenching all that meat with lemony fish sauce. He chewed and chewed, the meat sticking and unsticking to his teeth, the sound grating at everyone's ears, until Vinny couldn't take it anymore. He left the table and bounded in search of his cousin.

"Some dude has been in there for hella long," Darren said, when Vinny found him across the bathroom door, bathing in the muted yellow light and leaning against the wall. Phone in his hand, Darren had been refreshing his notifications, repeatedly, to no effect or news.

"That's no good," Vinny said. "You think it's the food? My pop's gonna be in for it, then."

"It's definitely the food. This is Battambang Bai."

Vinny leaned onto the wall opposite Darren, hands in his pockets. They stared at each other in silence.

"What do you think of, like—everything?" Vinny asked.

"I'm annoyed, if I'm gonna be honest. What part of this fucking situation is even for real?"

"You gotta have hope, bruh," Vinny said.

"What does hope have to do with our inheritance?"

"Dude, money's nothing but hope printed green."

"Yeah, well, that just means our hope is lost, too."

"That's why we gotta go find it. This is urgent, man, don't you see?"

Inadvertently, Darren slammed his head back and against the wall. "Fuck, that hurt."

At the end of the hallway, Soramee propped open the door to the alley and then exited with two heaping bags of trash. Sunlight stretched into the building, searing a blunt white onto the brown rug, just reaching the two cousins' feet. Soramee lingered outside, pacing and smoking a cigarette.

"Ever think about how, in Khmer," Vinny said, fixed on the crusty ceiling light, "Mas always be saying 'che nyum nou?' Like, 'Damn you know how to eat that real authentic shit, right there?' Like you can't just eat something, you gotta develop the skill to enjoy, taste, savor it, you know, really appreciate it, and if you don't have the skill, those Mas and their words, it's almost a sly shaming, because they'll just say it, like, 'che nyum nou,' like, this is a test, and the test forces you to swallow and smile and say that secret password, 'Bah, khnhom che, Ma,' and then feel like a fraud, a damn fool. Even if you don't feel strongly either way, even if you don't even hate it, even if you actually are digging the flavor but you're hesitant cause it's all still new, you have to just outright say, 'Yes, I am skilled at eating this,' because you're supposed to live up to that standard, you know? And that's pretty crazy, a mindfuck, don't you think?"

"Are you paraphrasing a new song?" Darren half-joked.

"I'm trying to tell you I fuck guys," Vinny said. He hovered off the wall, onto his toes, and fell back with a soft thud.

"Oh."

"Like, not only guys, but a lot of guys. I mean a lot of everyone, not just even guys or girls."

"Why are you telling me this now?" Darren asked, flush with an inward anger, at his stupid self, for not just accepting his cousin's admission.

"Because, man, we're gonna be business partners," Vinny said. "We're partners in crime now, on that Ming Peou level of gangsta, and, hopefully, then we'll be stage buddies . . . I haven't forgotten. I know we watched our auntie go up in flames, but I'm still holding you to that proposition, man. So, we can't have the unspoken stuff bringing us down. That's bad karma, and I think we're gonna need all the karma, all that good shit, to settle this money situation."

"If the money even exists."

"Why wouldn't it?"

Darren had no response. Because he did trust his Ming Peou. Of course he did.

"I'm sorry I didn't tell you," Vinny said. "I guess I wanted to get good at it first, you know, develop those skills. I didn't wanna be caught with a dick in my mouth, having to commit to being che at gay stuff and feeling like a goddamn phony. I don't know if that makes any sense. This all sounded, like, poetic and shit, in my head."

"Contrary to literally everything that's going on right

now," Darren said, "you don't need to prove anything. Not to me, that is."

"That means a lot."

"Should we hug?"

"Man, you know I'm always down for a body squeeze."

Vinny opened his arms, and Darren fell into his embrace. "I think I'm the one who's supposed to hug you. I'm supposed to pat your back and say shit like, Everything's gonna be okay. I'm proud of you. I don't see you as any different. You'll always be my pussy-loving cousin, but throw some dicks in there."

"Shit's warped at the moment, anyway."

Just then, Molly approached them. "How many times do you guys have to do this a week?"

"Vinny just told me he likes dick," Darren said, and the two boy cousins squeezed each other harder, swaying, rocking, laughing. "Or he likes his dick in other dudes," he added. "We haven't gotten into the specifics yet. But I'm still a proud gay role model."

"Great, you can teach him how to troll Grindr," Molly said. "You know, after we solve our shitshow of an inheritance."

"I'm afraid Grindr can't wait," Darren said.

"Seriously?" Molly said. "You're still skeptical about all the insane stuff that's been happening?"

"No," Darren said. "I'm in it now, unfortunately. What the fuck else am I gonna do?"

Vinny released his cousin. "Fuck, yes," he said, "we smoking a celebratory joint right after I take a piss!"

"Of course," Darren said.

"Someone's in the bathroom?" Molly said, rolling her eyes.

"Yeah, it's been forever," Darren said.

The cousins stared at the locked door, its peeling white paint, the water stains spreading into traces of greenish mold. It occurred to them how familiar they found restaurants like this, bathrooms marked with overuse, grocery stores that organized fresh desserts with dead fish, strip malls with little parking. And it occurred to them how this familiarity frayed at the edge of knowing, true knowing.

Outside, Soramee finished her cigarette. She reentered Battambang Bai and closed the door at the end of the hallway, extinguishing that solar glare. She considered the cousins with a wry distance, a sympathy toward their hopeful immaturity. She remembered being their age, not so long ago, at the turning point of adulthood, back when she'd told herself it would only be temporary, living at home, helping her parents pay their debts. Walking up to the cousins, she asked politely for them to move away from the bathroom. Then she pressed her shoulder against the flimsy wood, shook the bronze knob aggressively, forcing the door open to reveal an unoccupied toilet. "There you go," she said, and disappeared into the kitchen.

"Fuck, we're idiots," Darren said.

And Vinny said, "This is hilarious."

But Molly only shook her head. She stepped around them, through the open door, because she was just so tired of waiting, and Darren and Vinny shrugged. They were ready to cooperate, even as their inheritance, what that word even meant, began to unspool into loose, intangible threads, entangling with their hesitations, their uncertainties, and spilling all over Cambotown, too.

BABY YEAH

NONFICTION, ORIGINALLY PUBLISHED IN n+1

The semester prior to his suicide, my friend and I spent afternoons lounging around on a defective, footless sofa I had borrowed without any intention of returning. I was either going to donate it to Goodwill or steal the cushions and trash the frame, leaving it in a dumpster somewhere to collect vile rot. Early that same autumn, right as the heat was lifting, the owner, a classmate of ours, who had held on to the sofa's feet, had been exposed to our graduate program as morally corrupt in ways that were so hysterical that his sins appeared at once devastating and cosmic. For that reason, and because he had bullied my friend the previous academic term, during our first year as unofficial residents of Central New York, I had an intense desire for the owner to endure punishments of every order, whether severe or frivolous or petty.

But so on. The dusty air blasted through the expired filters my scummy landlord had lied about changing, while down on the sofa, we deluded ourselves into thinking we could somehow switch gears from digressive conversation into mature productivity. That didn't work out, so instead, we listened to Pavement's entire discography on shuffle on Spotify. If you haven't spent time with the band's five albums and nine EPs and four extended reissues or explored the rabbit holes of their underrated B sides, you might register this sonic experience as little more than the disjointed racket of pretentious slackers obsessed, for no apparent reason, with borderline nonsensical indie rock of the 1990s. I am embarrassed to confess that that was exactly the kind of art we studied and emulated.

My friend and I saw each other as hopeless writers, misunderstood prophets, critics of our cultural moment who rejected obvious and reductive politics. We never indulged the ordinary pursuits because we yearned to write masterpieces, timeless works infused with nihilistic joy and dissenting imaginations. We believed in our vision and our aesthetic, so when Stephen Malkmus crooned, "wait to hear my words and they're diamond-sharp / I could open it up," in the song "In the Mouth a Desert," we swore those lyrics spoke to us directly, spiritually, as though Pavement embodied a celestial mode of offbeat artistic creation.

At the same time, we remained detached from our lofty ambitions, skeptical of our dreams. We knew what we were, after all, which was graduate students scammed into university contracts with subpar health insurance. We lived off measly stipends and soggy pizza left over from department meetings. We taught undergrads we pitied in composition classes we hated, and we had an excessive tally of opinions that chafed our superiors. For example: We preferred grammar to metaphors. We considered Frank Ocean a better poet than Robert Hass—or Bob, as our famous professor called him—though we devoured his work, too. Like Malkmus, we thought of the sublime, of beauty, as muddled. "Heaven is a truck / It got stuck."

We were each "an island of such great complexity," as Malkmus sings in "Shady Lane/J vs. S." I wrote stories. My friend was a poet.

—

WE WERE FULL OF GIDDY potential, love for idiotic jokes, fuzzy notions begging to be clarified into true art, until one of us peered into the foreseeable future, or maybe the next gray day, and decided living wasn't worth the trouble.

—

WE MET DURING AN ORIENTATION for our MFA in creative writing, in a lecture hall inside a building shaped like a castle. My friend had on a *Wowee Zowee* T-shirt, and we immediately fell into a long argument about whether Pavement's underrated third album was its best. I've forgotten all the finer points and subtleties, but "AT&T" still hovers at the top of my list of favorite songs, so whoever was pro–*Wowee Zowee* was right. Mostly I can recall being aware of how insufferable we sounded. It was August 2017, and we were two baby-faced Millennials raving about the capricious music of Generation X.

My friend was fresh out of undergrad and had been raised dirt poor on the outskirts of Detroit, in that region of the poverty scale where the connecting threads of some people's kinship hardly make sense. His Iraqi Chaldean father had waltzed out of the obligations of parenthood years earlier and died a few years after that. The intimate history of his white mother, especially her shoddy employment record, was a topic my friend avoided elaborating on during social gatherings. Scattered between Michigan and West Virginia were siblings and half siblings and relatives, some outright refusing contact with other family members. He considered it miraculous that he'd stumbled into a bachelor's degree and then admission to a fully funded graduate program, let alone his true calling and poetic voice—a voice that would, time and time again, astonish me.

I identified with him immediately. Growing up, I wasn't *not* well-off—by the time I came along, my refugee parents had escaped their abysmal socioeconomic status—but I knew something about isolation and estrangement, from both the outer world and my insular community of Khmer Rouge genocide survivors and their children, none of them particularly empathetic to my queerness. Like me, my friend had assuaged his loneliness by pursuing a relationship with art—and music, in particular. And like him, I understood what it meant to come from a tough and bankrupt city, having weathered my childhood and adolescence in Stockton, California, home to the nation's third-largest Cambodian American population and, originally, Pavement and its band members. Both cities had been developed as prosperous hubs—Detroit the former automotive capital of the world, Stockton the bygone inland seaport of the California Gold Rush—and both had ended up degraded and depressed. So, we found visceral recognition in the rebellious and jubilant lyrics of "Box Elder," the scrappy, standout gem of *Slay Tracks: 1933–1969*, Pavement's debut EP: "Made me make a choice / That I had to get the fuck out of this town."

For years I listened to "Box Elder" oblivious to the fact that it was recorded in Stockton on January 17, 1989, the same day as the Cleveland School massacre, the decade's most fatal school shooting. When I discovered its uncanny connection to the massacre, I continued to listen to it anyway, armed with a willful disbelief. The connection went deeper: My mom, already traumatized by surviving the genocide, had witnessed the shooting at Cleveland Elementary. She worked as a bilingual aide, teaching ESL classes to the Southeast Asian kids, including the five killed and more than thirty maimed by the white gunman. The gunman, who killed himself before he could be arrested, imagined that his neighborhood had been invaded.

There weren't many people who could understand the specific cultural contexts my friend had experienced as a half-Iraqi Chaldean poet from the outskirts of Detroit. Not some of our peers in the graduate program, not the other writers we knew who represented so-called marginalized communities, and not the counselors and psychiatrists employed by Syracuse University. We're minorities within minorities, I'd often repeat to my friend, in an attempt to subdue his frustration with the compounding obstacles of his life.

Without trying, my friend and I challenged what people think of as normal American minorities—and, for that matter, normal writers enrolled in an MFA program. Or, at least it appeared that way. We came to writing late in college, as first-generation students, and had no parents or mentors or well-meaning high school teachers who'd cared to nurture our existential creativity. Our unknowing mothers stuffed us with junk food and bad television. He worked shitty jobs throughout his undergraduate career, busing tables for a while at a café owned by a racist Thai couple. I spent my adolescence at the beck and call of my parents, who always required assistance at our car repair shop. Obtaining a driver's license was less a feat of youthful freedom than a qualification to chauffeur customers to their homes, to shuttle younger cousins back and forth from school, to escort my grandmother to her appointments with the one Khmer and Khmer-speaking doctor in town, to sacrifice precious study hours during weeknights to help my father load and unload heavy equipment and auto parts. From an early age, my duty, like that of my older siblings and cousins, was to alleviate the pressures of sustaining my community's livelihood in the shadow of war and genocide and two million deaths—a quarter of Cambodia's population in 1975.

Even so, my friend and I tried to resent no one. We adopted an aura of queerness described by José Esteban Muñoz in *Cruising Utopia* as "a mode of 'being-with' that defies social conventions and conformism and is innately heretical yet still desirous for the world." We were hungry for connection, a constant state of "being-with," as others failed to empathize with us, and we failed to act normal.

This was why we idolized Pavement, with its albums distorted by lo-fi static. The band's reckless chords resisted the gloss of conventional rhythms. Its lyrics captured the chaotic feelings of being jaded yet bighearted, doubtful yet sentimental—feelings my friend and I thought were missing from literature, culture, perhaps even the world.

The first time we met, I wondered if he was gay. I'd be kidding myself if I said I didn't immediately notice his handsome beauty; the way his dark, wavy hair called to mind an earnest, self-conscious Louis Garrel; that he had broad shoulders but never cared to stand or sit upright. I appreciated that he wasn't freakishly ripped, even though he taught me how to curl biceps more effectively than what I'd picked up at the YMCA. Later on, I learned that he had a deep appreciation for male beauty and that he worshipped women, fell for them hard. He dreamed of cool chicks who'd grant him unwavering self-confidence. He spent months reading a Joni Mitchell biography he kept forgetting under the passenger seat of my car, a 2000 Honda Accord. He was always leaving his belongings there: his backpack, overpriced water bottles, and, one time, a wedge of gouda.

Men, it turned out, had no sexual effect on my friend, despite his mother's frequent claims that he was a *fruitcake*. Still, I thought his spirit was queer, the same way I associate Pavement with the flamboyant subversions of snarky glam rockers—notwithstanding the nerdy, ill-fitting clothes and the cheeky disillusionment so intrinsic to the residents of California's drought-ridden, agricultural Central Valley. "Queerness is that thing that lets us feel that this world is not enough," Muñoz writes, "that indeed something is missing." Without a doubt, hanging with my friend, you perceived the world as too small, too limited, too shortsighted. You'd think—or maybe this was only me—that society had to be operating in profoundly inexcusable ways if no secure place existed for him to thrive in.

—

ONE OCTOBER DAY, DURING THE semester before my friend committed suicide, we were planning the undergraduate composition classes we were teaching and, as usual, listening to the jagged sounds of Pavement. It was another lazy afternoon, unremarkable until a B side, which neither of us recognized, started playing off my laptop.

A live recording of a concert, the track starts with a simple progression of notes on the guitar, high to low, a brief downward cascade, as the crowd applauds the previous song. The guitarist produces variations of this progression, displaced into lower and lower octaves. A steady drumming creeps into the melody, and words trickle in: "Baby, baby, baby yeah," that last exclamation stretching into a prolonged drawl. Malkmus repeats the clause five times over, each iteration of *yeah* sustaining more of his breath, the tempo increasing through a rapturous crescendo until his singing explodes into painful howling and *baby* drops from the lyrics as *yeah* gets shouted, repeatedly but never monotonously, his voice blasting as loud against the atmosphere as it can reach.

After an eighth and final yelling of *yeah*, the final third of the recording transitions into its most legible lyrics: "It's torn, torn clean apart," Malkmus sings. A few seconds later, the song stops. The crowd cheers and claps. "This is our last song—it goes out to Sonic Youth," Malkmus announces before the recording stops, abruptly, like a stern father killing the vibe by yanking the stereo cord right out of the bedroom wall.

—

MY FRIEND AND I LISTENED to this three-minute B side, from the redux reissue of *Slanted and Enchanted*, with rapt attention. The escalating succession of *baby* and *yeah* drew us out of our lesson planning and forced us to sit there and wait patiently, suspended in Malkmus's straining voice, his fragmentary lyrics, until the song cohered into euphoria. But the promised catharsis never occurred, and when the ending arrived, almost as a jokey afterthought, after that sudden and literal *stop*, my friend and I just stared at each other. Then we burst into laughter.

Maybe I am overinflating this memory, which comes back to me often, persistently, in the aftermath of his suicide. Still, something about our introduction to "Baby Yeah" felt primal. That song unlocked within us some unbridled, unpretentious, mysterious feeling.

I want to ascribe precise meaning to that feeling, or at least I'll try to. Baby yeah: an affirmation of what remains unsaid, for something that doesn't yet exist. Baby yeah: a seductive and sentimental call for human connection. Baby yeah: a tender, riotous cry of wishful passion.

Another short B side was already halfway done by the time my friend and I had finished laughing. I had the sensation of being exposed, open and receptive to my surroundings, as though I were "torn clean apart." I felt complete with genuine affection for him.

We turned up the volume and played "Baby Yeah" again.

—

MONTHS LATER, DURING WHAT WOULD become his last weeks of living, my friend was crashing on my floor every few nights, a twenty-dollar yoga mat the sole cushion beneath his body. Maybe if we had admitted to the precarious balance of his mental and physical state, I would've told him to crawl onto my bed. We could've lain head to toe, under my sheets, like kids at a sleepover.

But he never wanted to burden anyone with the slightest of inconveniences, so we pretended that his racing thoughts were all right, however false that sentiment rang. Neither of us owned up to the truth—that my friend chose to stay on my floor, and the floors and sofas of other classmates, too often for him to feel well rested or even okay. He hanged himself the day he retreated to his own apartment.

In one of our last conversations, I told him that I thought music was the least cool of the arts. We were making chana masala and fried chicken crusted with almond flour. I needed him to be healthy, high off sustenance. What's beautiful about music, I was saying, is that everyone can appreciate a good melody. Consider how, in the grand scheme of the universe, there's not much difference between the technical prowess of a high school loser in Honors Band and Stephen Malkmus singing wonky tunes on Pavement records. How music appears wherever you happen to be. How ubiquitous it is: Patti Smith crooning in a used-book store in the East Village; Chance the Rapper bouncing against the aisles of the Syracuse Trader Joe's; Whitney Houston serenading the dark corners of a dive bar. It made no sense to rely on your music taste—or, dear god, your skills—to elevate yourself to some higher cultural echelon. That could only upend the communal experience of listening.

This is why, I finally said, I don't give a fuck about anyone's goddamn band. And why I won't give a fuck about yours.

My friend began to crack up, but he soon settled into himself. After he was discharged from the psych ward of the local hospital—it was there that he showed me the scars from his first attempts to kill himself, which were, at the time, red and crisp and healing, his shame hiding behind his loose hospital gown, his bashful grin covered with his fingertips all shoved against one another—I kept trying to help him laugh.

—

WHEN MY FRIEND COMMITTED SUICIDE, successfully this time, I couldn't eat for days. I barely made it up or down the stairs without hyperventilating. My thoughts splintered into nonsense. I didn't trust myself to drive, and when I was forced to, in that first week of mourning, I found myself paralyzed in the parking lot before my doctor's appointment, listening to the same CD that had been lodged in the stereo of my Accord for over three years. My friend adored that mix, which had Lauryn Hill, New Order, and Half Japanese on it. He'd join me on my errands so he could hear "Doo Wop (That Thing)" with the windows rolled down.

I was grieving, that was obvious. But it was more than that. My organs seemed displaced from their proper locations, precariously stacked on top of one another in a dangerous way. Sirens were going off throughout my body, and my insides, my feelings, my thoughts, were all obstructed. Was I hungry? Was I hurting? And what of the murky torrent of entangled emotions that kept trying to slam its way out of my torso, that toiled away beneath my suffocating, impenetrable grief?

I lashed out at mourning classmates with cruelty or total disregard. It felt horrible and irresponsible to indulge in these retaliations without truly understanding them, though I wasn't even sure that my peers had registered them as such. Maybe my gut reactions were valid? I was hopelessly repressed, my grief having eclipsed other, equally pertinent feelings, good or bad, healthy or not. For weeks I carried within myself the desire to explode, to force a catharsis, but I remained too tired, too swollen with unexpressed impulses, to address my needs.

I'm sorry about the vagueness, the abstract language, but so on. The imprecision of my sensations frustrated me to the point of self-destruction. It grew, this internal blockage, this debilitating repression. It kept surging with no release in sight.

Okay, fine, a concrete anecdote: The day after my friend's death, a poetry professor invited our whole graduate program, about forty students, to mourn collectively at his house. The faculty provided the soggy pizza. There was seltzer for the recovering alcoholics and a fruit platter from Wegmans arranged on a table. The cold spring sky washed the living room in a pale light. Taking in the professor's bookcases and minimalist furniture, I saw flashes of bright, amorphous shapes, as though I were staring at the back of my eyelids. I felt an acute disassociation, due to the shock and also the consequences of what I'd been doing the night before. Thirty minutes before the associate program director called to tell me about my friend's suicide, I had stupidly ingested a sativa edible, potent with the promise of giggly awareness. The phone call launched me into a horrifying and surreal state that lasted through the night. Up until this point—until this furniture, until this gathering of people—I had confronted my friend's nonexistence mostly stoned.

We mingled and exchanged somber small talk for an hour, at which point our professors surprised the room with a counselor from the university church. The man instructed us to sit in a circle, atop and between the sofas, whose feet, I noticed, were sturdy and fastened to the floor. He asked everyone to share their stories or impressions of my friend. He wore a priest's outfit, jet black with the white collar; I wore a neon-blue-and-yellow windbreaker I had bought when I accompanied my friend on his first trip to New York City.

My professors and classmates offered their stories to the room. They sang their sorrows, called my friend a good guy, said that he was a talented poet, that he was handsome and charming in his pensive, shaggy demeanor. Sitting there, I couldn't bear the idea that others could reminisce so easily and fondly about him, even those classmates he had admired. I wanted to punch a memoirist for talking about the class in which he had given my friend a dose of headache medication. A violent inner rage flared and was swelling, my nerves produced jolts of numbness that crawled under my skin and terrorized every memory I was summoning, and my voice began to slice through everyone else's stories, my own stories fleeing the chaotic storm of my grief-stricken mind. I had decided that any memories that didn't belong to me amounted to a superficial display of empty condolences. They were performances and nothing more.

Eventually, my barrage of interjections brought the collective sharing to a halt. The counselor directed his knees toward me, placed his hands firmly on his own thighs. "Do you feel like you could've done more to help your friend?" he asked, repeating a question he had originally posed to the room. "No," I said, "I did everything I could." I explained my and my friend's last weeks together, intending to hammer into everyone a debilitating guilt for their negligence. "I want you to know," he responded, "you should be proud of being there for your friend, in his time of need." Tears glistened on the cheeks of the room. I was crying, too, but hated myself for doing that, for doing that there.

Later, as people dispersed and kept chewing and swallowing more pizza, the counselor pulled me into the entryway. We stood in a mess of shoes. He said he meant those words; really he did; he was being genuine and true. But my rage only compounded my grief, crowding my head with resentment.

It is easy to portray my behavior in this anecdote as mostly benign. It is also easy to assign my actions a sympathetic explanation, in the retrospective and mechanical way those things go. I felt abandoned by my friend. I felt guilty for not doing enough to support him. I was angry at those who had neglected his struggles. But if I'm being honest, I'll never fully understand the nebulous reality I inhabited while grappling with his suicide—all the designer drugs I consumed, the bursts of adrenaline sending me into fits of mania and then directly onto the floor, where I sobbed and heaved for hours, where my friend had spent so many nights. I can tell you only what I found helpful.

—

DURING THE WEEKS THAT FOLLOWED my friend's death, I awoke each morning, and from every cloudy nap, thinking, *Maybe it was all a dream*. A drug-induced nightmare. I checked my phone periodically to see if I'd received any signs of life, or rebirth. I ignored calls from relatives and messages from other people whom I later cut out of my life. I would tell a close acquaintance from college, a former best friend, to stop contacting me. Her life, I texted without remorse—her heteronormative relationship with her fiancé, who was yet another former friend of mine; her stupid engineering job at Google—had begun to disturb and disgust me.

Among the last texts I'd received from my friend was one about Fat Tony's album *Smart Ass Black Boy*, with the instructions to check out the song "BKNY feat. Old Money." I revisited this conversation one morning at the end of May, my mind hazy and incoherent. I laughed at the corniness of him texting me—whom he referred to as "Tony" or "Tone-Tone," since he bestowed a nickname on everyone he loved—a track by a rapper named Fat Tony. I inserted my AirPods and listened to "BKNY." When it ended, I hit Replay. And then, after four minutes, I hit the button again. And so on.

For two hours, I lay within the confines of "BKNY," having stepped inside the textured layers of Fat Tony's chill rapping, like the stoned narrator in the prologue to *Invisible*

Man descending into the depths of Louis Armstrong's "(What Did I Do to Be So) Black and Blue"—a record the narrator longs to hear on five phonographs all playing at once. In brief spurts, I remembered, truly or maybe in the closest approximation to the truth I'd experienced since his death, what it felt like to hang out with my friend, that surreal ease we embodied on some good days, with no responsibilities but writing sentences and lines of poetry, or simply hunting for inspiration. These were the days when we didn't take ourselves so seriously, as Millennial idiots getting paid to write, when we roamed the streets of downtown Syracuse laughing at nonsense: antagonistic looks from passersby, the trash caught in the heaps of yellowed snow, shiny wrappers of the junk food we'd inhaled as kids, how every upscale restaurant in Central New York believed pickled red onions could transform a dish into fine dining.

At which point, I turned to "Baby Yeah." The entirety of that afternoon and night, I journeyed through the depths of the song, which I set on repeat. I dissolved into a deeper and deeper sadness with each repeat—not the grief of my past few weeks, the disorientation traversing the eternal distance between me and my dead friend, but the melancholy of sinking into myself by virtue of my newfound willingness to embrace those memories he had left behind. Tentatively, and then less so, I allowed my friend's presence to become reborn in my mind, for it to vanish, again and again, with every iteration of that downward melodic progression, of Malkmus lamenting "it's torn, torn clean apart," of that sudden and flippant invocation to *stop*. I was crying, I swear, harder than ever.

What is remembering other than revitalizing a corpse that will return to its grave? The memory always reaches a limit. Final frames of a reel that fade into depressing blankness. The more history you have with the deceased, the more endings you will suffer through.

If emotions are the waverings of the mind, then the overwhelming experience of grief, and all the frustration it produces, can spin you into madness, a dreadful internal force thrashing against the walls of your mind, your body, your spirit. How do you escape? Perhaps by spinning so hard into the truth that you collapse.

—

EVEN NOW, MORE THAN A year after my friend's death, I will listen to "Baby Yeah" on a loop, though not for nearly as long as I did in those first months of mourning, when the song could go on for weeks. "Difference lies between two repetitions," writes Gilles Deleuze in *Difference and Repetition*. (Stephen Malkmus recommended another book of his, *A Thousand Plateaus: Capitalism and Schizophrenia* [cowritten with Félix Guattari], in *Artforum*. But so on.) "The role of the imagination," Deleuze continues, "or the mind which contemplates in its multiple and fragmented states, is to draw something new from repetition, to draw difference from it."

Repetition allows for reinvention. I am rereading Deleuze's words as I parse the enigmatic purpose of my obsessive listening. I wonder if the repetition of "Baby Yeah," and the retelling of the tender history it evokes, and the echoing of each *baby* and each yelled *yeah*—if all this enables fresh understandings, radical feelings never before experienced that can dismantle the blockage, or at least replace it with something else. Perhaps this is Friedrich Nietzsche's notion of the eternal return, which Deleuze describes as the "power of beginning and beginning again," and I'm confirming for myself that regardless of the infinite suicides I might witness, regardless of how doomed and nauseating modern civilization might be (at least according to Nietzsche), I would always choose to relive those awesome, brutal years with my friend.

And, yes, I do think my friend also grasped the power of repetition. Why else did he submit to those undying dreams of his own limitations?

The January preceding his suicide, he emailed me the last poem he would finish. Actually, he sent it three separate times within the span of ten minutes, having made the slightest of revisions. "Avec Amour" ends:

> . . . the other night I passed by the outdoor pool
> where I swam every morning the summer
> my first girlfriend
> moved to Japan,
>
> and I noticed how the snow almost seemed
> to be falling out of the moon
> as if it were a hole leading to another day,
> another hour in the past
>
> made of nothing and causing
> everything.

It's possible that "Baby Yeah" guides me to "another hour in the past" I cannot otherwise access. The song could be "made of nothing and causing everything," the way I keep my friend alive in my imagination, the way I allow him, finally, to die. Maybe he needed to know, simply and practically, that he could stumble upon portals other than the lifeless moon, or even will them into existence.

My favorite sentence in *Difference and Repetition* reads, "All our rhythms, our reserves, our reaction times, the thousand intertwinings, the presents and fatigues of which we are composed, are defined on the basis of our contemplations." I want to share this with my friend. I wish I could reassure him that his presents and fatigues are valid. Yes, they inform your rhythms. But—please, hear me out—don't you think difference breathes in the expanses that lie amid your monotonous thoughts? Even as you see in the future only suicide, your mind fosters so many novel meanings that are essential, rabbit holes leading to unknown hours and possibilities, and maybe if you wait, for just a bit longer, these meanings will bleed into your being, restructuring the reserves of your spirit, and maybe then, after a serious exploration of all that is true, you, my dear friend, will feel something akin to new.

ABOUT ANTHONY VEASNA SO

ANTHONY VEASNA SO (1992–2020) was a graduate of Stanford University and earned his MFA in fiction at Syracuse University. His story collection, *Afterparties*, a *New York Times* bestseller, was long-listed for the Andrew Carnegie Medal for Excellence in Fiction, and won both the Ferro-Grumley Award for LGBTQ Fiction and the National Book Critics Circle's John Leonard Prize for Best First Book. His writing has appeared in *The New Yorker, The Paris Review, n+1, Granta,* and ZYZZYVA. A native of Stockton, California, he taught at Colgate University, Syracuse University, and the Center for Empowering Refugees and Immigrants in Oakland, California.

ABOUT JONATHAN DEE

JONATHAN DEE is the author of eight novels, most recently *Sugar Street*. His novel *The Privileges* was a finalist for the 2011 Pulitzer Prize and the winner of the 2011 Prix Fitzgerald and the St. Francis College Literary Prize. A former contributing writer for *The New York Times Magazine*, a senior editor of *The Paris Review*, and a National Magazine Award–nominated literary critic for *Harper's Magazine* and *The New Yorker*, he has received fellowships from the National Endowment for the Arts and the Guggenheim Foundation. He is the director of the graduate writing program at Syracuse University.